Will Cycle be Unbroken?

Churches of Christ
Face the 21st Century

Douglas A. Foster

A·C·U PRESS
Abilene, Texas

Article on p. 41 reprinted with permission from The Door magazine (issue
#1190, Box 530, Yreka, California 96097
Printed in the United States of America
ISBN 0-89112-013-0
Library of Congress Card Number 94-78830

2,3,4,5

Dedicated to

Linda, my wife,

Mary Elizabeth and Mark, my children,

Ralph and Lisabeth, my parents,

and

my teachers at Mars Hill Bible School

Contents

Will the Cycle be Unbroken?

Northern Alabama has been a stronghold of Churches of Christ[1] for well over one hundred years. According to 1990 data, almost 100 congregations exist in Colbert and Lauderdale counties alone, with a membership of nearly 14,000.[2] I was born in Colbert County in 1952, and it was there that I came to faith in Christ.

Churches of Christ are generally known for their theological conservatism, and Churches of Christ in North Alabama are among the most conservative of all. Before my tenth birthday I became aware of the fighting still going on in our anti-institutional controversy. A running battle between two papers, *The Contender* and *The Defender,* kept the dispute hot for years.

Yet those problems by no means dominate my religious memories. For twelve years I was nurtured in the shadow of T. B. Larimore's homeplace as I attended the namesake of his nineteenth-century academy—Mars Hill Bible School. There is no doubt that Mars Hill was a most thorough school in "the things surely believed among us." Yet the daily Bible classes and chapel services were remarkably positive in their emphasis on simple biblical Christianity. The quarrels then plaguing the churches found little place in our studies.

After those twelve years came four at David Lipscomb University, followed by short teaching assignments at B. C. Goodpasture Christian School in Madison, Tennessee, and Ezell-Harding Christian School in Antioch, Tennessee. Along with that work were almost ten years as Associate Minister of the Jackson Park Church of Christ in Nashville. Then followed seven years teaching in the history department of David Lipscomb University and, most recently, an appointment to teach church history at Abilene Christian University. My entire life's experience has been with and for members of Churches of Christ.

I recognize that these experiences do not make me any more qualified than many others to make statements about the matters in this book. In fact, my experiences make it more difficult to be as objective as I might wish. Nevertheless, my heritage and background have given me intimate knowledge of the Churches of Christ in the United States. That knowledge, along with study of Scripture and church history, has hopefully provided some tools for placing our current situation into the larger context in which I believe it must be understood.

Today, Churches of Christ are troubled by a number of controversies that have inflamed old wounds and opened new ones. We are not now, nor have we ever been, unaffected by the events and ideas of the world in which we live. The scriptural ideal is not to be "of the world," yet we are in the world and we must grapple with its influences.

Decades ago, sociologists and historians of

religion identified a process called the "sect-to-church" progression. Described by the German scholar Ernst Troeltsch in his 1912 study *The Social Teaching of the Christian Church,* and refined and expanded in 1929 by H. Richard Niebuhr in *The Social Sources of Denominationalism,* the process involves stages through which all religious movements tend to move. A period of initial fervor and exclusivity is followed by a stable consolidating phase. Finally, the body settles into a respectable position in the larger religious world, but without its early vibrancy and success. The final stage involves decline that could ultimately lead to the body's death.

Are Churches of Christ locked into this seemingly inescapable pattern? Are we in a period of decline? Warnings of such a possibility are not new. In 1976 Batsell Barrett Baxter urged

> We must recognize that people and institutions grow old, get tired, become lazy and die. We see this happening in our own life-cycles and the life-cycles of those all around us. Tragically, the same tendency is also seen in movements. There is a period of vigor in the early years, followed by decline and ultimate disappearance. This must not happen to the Restoration Movement."[3]

If we are already in this pattern, what, if anything, can be done to stop it? That is what this book is about. Will the cycle of decline and division be unbroken in Churches of Christ?

Deep respect and love for my religious heritage and its roots in Scripture and the Spirit of Scripture prompted the writing of this book. I cherish the hundreds of thousands of God's people in Churches of Christ. I am part of the Churches of Christ and will remain so. This book is intended to build us up in

Christ, not to attack and destroy. Yet, as is always the case when we seriously examine ourselves, we may have to relinquish understandings that hinder us from being the people God would have us be.

Dozens have helped with this volume, and I am extremely grateful to all of them. David Howard of the David Lipscomb University Library helped supply information on the periodicals of our movement and encouragement in early stages of the work. I received feedback from several Christian college presidents thanks to Harold Hazelip, who gave me the opportunity to present some of the preliminary material to them. In addition, I have received valuable suggestions from colleagues who have read chapters or drafts of chapters. Special thanks are due Leonard Allen, Ted McAllister, Kerry Anderson, Bill Leonard, Tom Olbricht, Dub Orr, Steve Weathers, John York, Mike Cope, Darryl Tippens and Jack Reese. My ACU graduate assistants, Chris Heard and Rick Cobb, did much leg work while gathering information for chapters.

In the process of writing this book I had to come to grips with a fact that I suppose every author faces—you can't say everything about every topic. You can't even say everything about one topic. There are many other things that need to be said. But a book has to end at some point, as imperfect as it may be. I pray that the things I have said will build us up in Christ Jesus. I pray that, however insufficient and incomplete this effort is, it will help us understand ourselves and move on to an ever-greater future in God's service.

I am grateful to the hundreds of people who have influenced the ideas in this book through their writing and speaking over the last decade. You will see many of their names in the notes. I have tried to be honest in the statement of their ideas and clear in my own statements.

And now, in the words of T. B. Larimore, "Criticize freely, brethren [and sisters]. I will not retaliate." Some of the judgments in this study will undoubtedly have to be modified as we move into the future. But I am convinced that Churches of Christ are moving into an era of ever greater service to God. The point of the book is to urge each of us individually and all of us together to seek first the kingdom of God and his righteousness, so that all our needs may be met by him. My sincere desire is that this book will contribute to the self-understanding of Churches of Christ and to true spiritual renewal within the will of God.

Abilene, Texas
September 30, 1994

Endnotes

[1] I know that some are uncomfortable with terms like "our heritage," "Restoration Movement churches," or even "Churches of Christ." That fear is legitimate—we cannot equate our immediate heritage or anyone else's with the universal church of God in all times and places. I have tried to deal with that issue in chapter three, which is about our self-concept.

[2] Statistics gathered by Mac Lynn for *Churches and Church Membership in the United States 1990* (Atlanta: Glenmary Research Center, 1992), 38, 41. See also Lynn, *Churches of Christ in the United States* (Nashville: Gospel Advocate Company, 1991), 1-32.

[3] Batsell Barrett Baxter, "The Crisis," unpublished speech delivered August 17, 1976, Abilene Texas. Transcript in Herald of Truth collection in the David Lipscomb University Library.

Church of Christ: Organized by Presbyterians in Kentucky in 1804 and in Pennsylvania in 1809. 1.6 million followers. The New Testament is believed in and what is written in the Bible is followed without elaboration; rites are not ornate; baptism is of adults. *The New York Public Library Desk Reference,* 1989, 192.

What makes this brief listing so significant is the fact that as recently as ten years ago, the Churches of Christ would likely not have rated even a mention in such an important reference work, except perhaps as a radically conservative offshoot of the Christian Church (Disciples of Christ). True, it is not the first time we have received national attention. From the mid-fifties through the sixties, Churches of Christ were noted as one of the fastest growing religious bodies in America, though likely based on inaccurate data.[1] Yet in Sydney Ahlstrom's 1972 award-winning text, *A Religious History of the American People,* Churches of Christ are portrayed as odd exclusivists who split from the Disciples over issues that make no sense to the rest of the Christian world.[2]

What has brought us from being described as an aberrant offshoot of the Disciples to being the sole example of the Stone-Campbell Restoration Movement in the *New York Public Library Desk Reference?* There are several possible answers to the question. Some might attribute the switch to the decline in numbers among Disciples over the past decades—almost one million members lost since the mid-1960's. Churches of Christ may simply be more significant numerically than the other major "branches" of the Restoration Movement.[3]

In the scholarly world, attention has been focused on Churches of Christ and restorationism through the work of Richard Hughes and Leonard Allen. Their book, *Illusions of Innocence* (University of Chicago Press, 1988), places the idea of restorationism or primitivism into a larger American context, showing its importance for American history and thought. Significant essays from a 1985 Conference on American Primitivism held at Abilene Christian University have been published, again placing the movement into its larger context.[4]

Popular books aimed at members of Churches of Christ have paralleled these scholarly works. *The Worldly Church* showed how Churches of Christ were as susceptible as any group to the allures of our culture and society. Our roots in Enlightenment thought were exposed and criticized in a sharp but caring way. *Discovering Our Roots* showed that the Stone-Campbell Restoration Movement was not the only restoration movement. The idea of restoring primitive Christianity has been common in many religious movements across the globe and throughout history, each with its own understanding of what to restore.

Major historical and religious journals have published reviews of these books.[5] In addition, Richard Hughes organized a major Conference on Primitivism in June 1991 at Pepperdine University, from which another book of essays is to be published. These publications and events have undoubtedly served to draw attention to Churches of Christ.

All this attention on our heritage and identity, from both inside and out, has prompted many to reflect on who we are. That can be a healthy process. Yet there is something disturbing about all this scrutiny that is difficult to escape. Church historian Ted Campbell expressed this unsettling feeling in an article on nostalgia. "The critical study of a tradition does not ensure its life; in fact, the critical study of a tradition may well be the sign of its death." Decrying the problems of his own Methodist tradition, Campbell muses, "We are, I'm afraid, more intellectuals than evangelists. And, as realistic as I wish to be as a historian, I'd confess to a certain degree of nostalgia in my work. Perhaps only a sense of tragic loss can compel the urgent search for one's roots."[6]

Is this sense of tragic loss behind the scholarly scrutiny and the alarmed cries of danger among Churches of Christ? Do we as a body have a clear focus on who we were, who we are, and whom we must become to truly be people of God? Nostalgia has definitely set in among some of us. Many long for something that used to be, for better days, now seen as slipping away, when "we stood for something." What is that "something"? Is it the proud confidence that we were "right" and the "only ones going to heaven?" Is it our reputation for knowing the Scriptures better than any other religious group? Is it the certainty that "denominationalism" was wrong and that we were not a denomination? Is it the conviction that we had restored the church of the New Testament?

Nostalgia in an organization is an indication that something is wrong.[7] Mentally healthy people cannot live in the past—but they must deal with their past in a constructive way before they can move on. For us the crucial question is whether the things for which some are nostalgic are helps or hindrances to our attempts to know and conform to God's will—to restore individuals to a right relationship to God.

This book is not intended to provide complete answers to every problem now troubling Churches of Christ. It is meant to prompt us to take a serious look at ourselves and what might happen if current trends continue. It contains a message of hope for the future—that the cycles of decline and division so familiar to the religious world are *not* inevitable—when we allow God's power to work in us. The key for each of us as individuals and as members of Churches of Christ is to put allegiance to God first and foremost. It is the task of this book to help us see ourselves as we are so that we can become the kind of people we ought to be.

Endnotes

[1]Mac Lynn's systematic data collection on Churches of Christ reported in *Churches and Church Membership in the United States 1980* (Atlanta: Glenmary Research Center, 1982), 2 showed slightly over 1.2 million members. This was half of what had been estimated previously. Earlier figures were evidently based primarily on anecdotal estimations.

[2] Sydney E. Ahlstrom, *A Religious History of the American People* (New Haven: Yale University Press, 1972), 822-823.

[3] *Churches and Church Membership 1990,*1 shows membership as follows: Christian Church (Disciples of Christ), 677,223; Christian Churches and Churches of Christ (also called Independent Christian Churches), 966,976; Churches of Christ, 1,280,838.

[4] Richard T. Hughes, ed. *The American Quest for the Primitive Church* (Urbana: University of Illinois Press, 1988).

[5] Martin E. Marty, "Sophisticated Primitives Then, Primitive Sophisticates Now," *Christian Century* 106(June 7-14, 1989):588-591 reviews *Illusions of Innocence* and *The American Quest for the Primitive Church;* Mark A. Knoll, "Rethinking Restorationism—A Review Article," *The Reformed Journal* 39(November 1989):15-21 adds *Discovering Our Roots* and *The Worldly Church* to the list. Reviews of one or more of the books appeared in journals ranging from *Baptist History and Heritage* to *Restoration Quarterly* and from *Catholic Historical Review* to the *Journal of Church and State.*

[6] Ted Campbell, "Is It Just Nostalgia? The Renewal of Wesleyan Studies," *Christian Century* 107(April 18, 1990):398.

[7] See Robert Dale, *To Dream Again* (Nashville: Broadman Press, 1980), 105-16.

Will the Cycle be Unbroken?

Chapter 1

Cycles of Growth, Decline and Division in American Churches

Not since the long and painful split between the Churches of Christ and Christian Churches, acknowledged in the 1906 religious census, has our fellowship faced such wrenching division. True, there have been other times of tension. The premillennial and non-institutional controversies of the1930's and 1950's disturbed Churches of Christ. Those fights, however, resulted in relatively small divisions. At the end of the twentieth century, Churches of Christ face a major crisis—one that threatens to shatter the fellowship into multiple factions.

We in Churches of Christ have tended to view our internal affairs as unique and fundamentally different from what goes on in the larger religious world. Unquestionably we are unique in important ways. What we too often have failed to realize is that we are subject to the same social and cultural influences that affect all organizations composed of humans.

Affluence and poverty, racial attitudes, education levels, population shifts, wars, power struggles, and countless other factors affect the success or failure of churches.

Certainly we cannot treat Christ's church as a mere sociological or historical object. Yet sociological and historical matters are vital to our identity, and understanding them is important for dealing responsibly with our current situation. We must keep reminding ourselves that God is ultimately in charge—it is His church, not ours. Yet if we ignore or misunderstand the matters in this chapter, we will likely aggravate our problems. God does not promote ignorance.

The aim of this chapter is to begin to understand how Churches of Christ fit into the larger context of American religion by focusing on historic cycles of religious growth, decline and division. What does it mean to talk about historical and sociological cycles? Cycles are trends or patterns of events that occur in all organizations—including religious bodies. Such cycles are not inevitable. If they were, there would be no reason to write a book like this. The point is, unless we understand something about the normal life cycle of organizations and, relying on God's power, take steps to avoid destructive trends, we can and will be drawn into the whirlpool of decline and division.

This world is not our ideal home. It is under the sway of God's enemy and subject to principalities and powers of darkness (Eph. 6:12). The cycles characteristic of the world are often designed to draw us individually and collectively toward spiritual destruction. The Lord of the universe, however, can keep us from danger by his power. He can reverse the trends and break the destructive cycles if we submit to him, allowing him to live in and work through us (Eph. 3:20).

Life Cycles of Religious Movements

Twentieth century sociologists and historians of religion have attempted to identify how religious bodies develop and what makes them succeed or fail.[1] One of the most important early studies was written by German theologian Ernst Troeltsch. He described what became a standard understanding of the "sect to church" development. In *The Social Teachings of the Christian Churches*, Troeltsch defined a "church" as an officially established body that takes in everyone at birth and makes claims over all society. Leaders strictly maintain correct doctrine and forms of worship, but individual religious commitment and moral responsibility are not so important. A "sect," in contrast, separates itself almost entirely from society and emphasizes the total commitment of the individual members to the teachings and practices of the group.

Troeltsch was describing the European situation with which he was familiar—official state churches contrasted with exclusive groups of dissenters who viewed the state church as polluted and evil. Examples include the Church of England vs. the English Baptists or Methodists, and the German Lutheran Church contrasted with Anabaptist groups like the Mennonites. Most important for our discussion, Troeltsch explained that "sects" tend to lose their exclusivist edge over time and become more like the "church" in their acceptance of and claims over society. In other words, "sects" eventually change so that

3

they fit into their culture. They no longer protest against it—they become part of it!

Scholars of religion modified Troeltsch's categories to describe more accurately the American situation where there is no established church. Usually the term "denomination" is used for groups that are comfortable as part of the general culture of the nation. Yet Troeltsch's model of movement from sect to church (or denomination) is still widely accepted. Sociologists of religion observe that historically religious groups tend to move from strict separation from society to gradual acceptance of and accommodation to it.[2]

Wade Clark Roof and William McKinney, in an important 1987 study titled *American Mainline Religion*, reflect the "sect to church" theory in their observation that

> As sectarian religious groups achieved middle class status in the past, they have tended to move toward the theological and political middle. . . Upward mobility and a broadened membership base predispose religious bodies to more middle-class values; sectarian and exclusivist stances lose out to more accommodating, less dogmatic religious styles. That movement also generates strong counteractions and has been an important social source of religious schism. Division will continue to occur in the conservative Protestant camp as successive reactionaries attempt to resist the trends toward greater accommodations.[3]

The available data on Churches of Christ indicates that we fit this pattern. Our overall education level has increased steadily over the last several decades. Between the mid-1940's and the mid-1980's Churches of Christ moved from the lowest rank in overall socioeconomic status to the middle rank. These classifications are based on level of education, family income, occupational prestige, and perceived social class.[4] Some of our accommodations to culture and society's assumptions were laid bare in *The Worldly Church*. We saw that we, like society at large, had come to have little room for the mysterious and transcendent. Everything was understandable and controllable by the human mind.[5]

The point of this discussion is not to make a blanket condemnation of sociological moves from "sect" to "church." Temptations to pride and other grave sins exist whether a group is poor and rural or rich and urban. We must realize, however, that as changes in socioeconomic status take place, the dangers and temptations change too.

Growth, Decline and Division

Closely tied to the movement from sect to church are cycles of growth, decline and division. The following discussion is adapted from David Moberg's *The Church as a Social Institution: The Sociology of American Religion,* and represents a consensus view of the life-cycle stages of religious bodies, based on study of many groups.

The first stage is identified by deep, often emotional, dissatisfaction with the practices and beliefs of an existing church. The unrest eventually leads to a reform movement within the original body, usually under the leadership of one or more highly capable, energetic and convincing leaders. New beliefs and practices begin to set the group apart from the parent. Sociologists label this the "incipient organization" stage.

The "formal organization" stage follows immediately with the appearance of strong leadership.

5

The new group seeks to develop a clear identity and purpose. It distinguishes itself sharply from its former relationships and asks its followers to commit themselves totally to the group's goals. Members of the new movement create slogans and symbols to identify themselves. The leaders almost always begin as iconoclasts, lashing out at what they see as corruptions of true religion. They gradually moderate this harsh attitude, however, as the movement advances to the third stage of "maximum efficiency."

At this point thoughtful planning and organization replace the early passionate nature of the movement, and the leaders become statesmen instead of rebels. The offshoot lessens its hostility toward other groups, with the result that in the eyes of the larger community it begins to move from "despised sect" to near equality with other denominations. Rapid but uneven growth is often characteristic of this third stage. The dangers that come with such growth include failure to integrate new members properly and conflicting understandings of the nature of the group.

In the "institutional" phase, the church becomes a bureaucracy. Self-centered and self-perpetuating boards and committees come to run the organization with little sensitivity to the members, though demanding much from them. Worship becomes more ritualistic, membership standards are relaxed, feelings of intimacy decline, sermons often become lectures on social issues, and secular activities become a major focus of the week's activities.

The final stage of the cycle is "disintegration." Gradually, leaders become out of touch with the membership. There is an increase in formalism, absolutism, indifference and even corruption. This leads to half-hearted support by members, losses to other religious groups and formation of new sects, beginning the process all over again. Complete collapse may be the result, though some leaders and members might be able to restore the body through an internal renewal movement.[6] Social institutions naturally resist their own deaths. Members are almost always forced into some kind of adjustment for survival. The adjustment could revitalize the original church or generate a new organization from the ruins of the old.

This five-stage process is theoretical. Some groups move rapidly past one or more of the phases, while others seem to be stalled for long periods in one stage or even move back and forth between two phases. One thing is consistent, however. Institutions are constantly changing. Regardless of how much they try not to change or believe they have not changed, the one constant in human existence is change. Though Moberg proposes that it is possible to reverse the process described above, he admits that the sequence "grows out of natural patterns of cause-and-effect relationships that as yet have been explored only superficially."[7]

Several other models that describe the life cycle of organizations help us see other aspects of this complex process. Religious anthropologist Anthony F. C. Wallace described a group's development from a "steady state," or stable phase, to periods of increased individual stress and cultural distortion. This is followed by either disintegration or revitalization. Revitalization comes only when "prophetic" individuals in the group are able to move beyond old ways of thinking and acting to create a new vision. Revitalization movements succeed when they are able to overcome and adapt to resistance and persuade a significant number of people to embrace their new understandings. After revitalization comes another steady state.[8]

Still another useful view of the cycle is described in *Shaping the Coming Age of Religious Life*. Though focusing on Catholic communities, this description adds insightful analysis to the development seen in the other models. The authors depict periods of foundation, expansion, stabilization and breakdown. Finally, in what they label the critical period, the organization may become extinct, survive at a minimal level, or be revitalized. The authors observe that in those communities that are revitalized three factors have always been present: a transforming response to the signs of the times; a reappropriation of the kind of dedication, energy and vision characteristic of the founders; and a profound renewal of the life of prayer, faith, and Christ centeredness. Personal transformation and new insights concerning the group's purpose move leaders to focus on a new positive vision of the group's future.[9]

The history of the Restoration Movement in the nineteenth century reflects in a remarkable way the cycles we have just seen. The early leaders of the movement broke with their denominations over what they saw as religious tyranny. The denominational structures and creeds that had developed since the Reformation had become as oppressive and restrictive as any Luther, Zwingli, Calvin and others fought to change. Barton W. Stone, Thomas and Alexander Campbell, Walter Scott and other leaders of the "nineteenth-century Reformation" began a vibrant new movement calling people to leave creeds and clergy, relying on the Scriptures for their beliefs and practices. Slogans like "We speak where the Bible speaks and are silent where the Bible is silent," and "Christians only, but not the only Christians" identified them and contrasted their beliefs with those of their former associates. They were eager to reexamine long-held assumptions, to learn and grow as they studied anew the gospel message.

The iconoclasts became statesmen, however. Alexander Campbell himself eventually advocated a central organization for the movement. The annual convention and the American Christian Missionary Society served to give the movement a structure beyond the local congregation and led to the creation of other agencies and societies. It also served as a visible sign to some that the movement was moving away from its original ideals and needed a correction. A part of the movement came to feel alienated from the segment that supported the missionary society and other innovations. With their own leaders and slogans and a new zeal for standing for what they saw as the true basis of the original movement, the Churches of Christ took shape in the late 1800's and early 1900's.

Our congregational structure made the separation long and painful, yet we had clearly emerged as a separate group by the first decade of the new century. As the twentieth century progressed, we organized schools and other agencies. Controversy surrounded this organization and there was a split in the 1950's over church-sponsored institutions. Since the 1960's, however, there has been a growing alienation between those who fear that some in Churches of Christ are moving away from essential truths, and those open to new ideas about everything from Bible

9

study to worship styles. Tremendous stress surrounds the discussion of such issues as biblical interpretation, feminism and lines of fellowship, and no clear consensus exists. It appears that Churches of Christ have entered the "critical stage" or the period of cultural distortion and disintegration described above.

Perhaps the single most important understanding to get from these descriptions is that contrary to liberal notions, human beings cannot keep up constant development. We can't even maintain the status quo! Breakdown and disintegration are a part of the human condition that we cannot escape. Regardless of where Churches of Christ may be in the cycles described above, solutions to our problems will come only after humble acceptance of our own inabilities and recognition that God alone can supply us with what it takes to revitalize us in the midst of division and disintegration.[10]

Religious Division in America Today

A final pattern of division that has become increasingly evident in the twentieth century is described in detail in two influential studies by Robert Wuthnow of Princeton University. In *The Restructuring of American Religion* (Princeton, 1988) and *The Struggle for America's Soul* (Eerdmans, 1989), Wuthnow insists that neither the "Catholic, Protestant and Jew" division described by Will Herberg in the 1950's, nor the traditional denominational divisions are the most important lines now drawn in American religion. Particularly since World War II, two opposing camps have developed that cut directly through most religious bodies. He labels the two groups liberal and conservative. Quoting religious historian

Peggy Shriver, Wuthnow describes how each group views the other.

> Liberals abhor the smugness, the self-righteousness, the absolute certainty, the judgmentalism, the lovelessness of a narrow dogmatic faith. Conservatives scorn the fuzziness, the marshmallow convictions, the inclusiveness that makes membership meaningless—the 'anything goes' attitude that views even Scripture as relative. Both often caricature the worst in one another and fail to see the best.[11]

Wuthnow contends that this fragmentation has been taking place within denominations for several decades. In fact, denominations long identified as theologically liberal, like the United Church of Christ, the United Methodist Church, and the Christian Church (Disciples of Christ), all have grassroots conservative renewal movements in their ranks. Furthermore, traditionally conservative churches have spawned various kinds of progressive renewal groups.

A working definition of the terms *liberal* and *conservative* now will hopefully help avoid misunderstandings later. In the *most general* sense, the terms indicate a fundamental difference in understanding the nature of human beings. Liberalism is inherently optimistic about what human beings can do. The liberal attitude sees humans as able to solve all the problems that beset them. In the liberal view, all it takes is hard work, efficient use of abilities and education to insure continual advancement.

Conservatism is less optimistic about human nature and ability. In the extreme, conservatives view humans as fatally flawed, even depraved. They do not see human advancement as inevitable. Instead, they believe that the general trend is toward decline. The

11

important thing, in the conservative view, is to hold fast to cherished beliefs and practices which are seen as the truth.

Religious liberalism and conservatism became distinguished most sharply in the last couple of centuries as modern scientific thought undermined traditional Christian beliefs about the Bible and its authority. Liberals came to deny the unique inspiration and infallibility of Scripture which led to the denial of other foundational Christian beliefs.

Wuthnow's analysis is helpful as far as it goes. He does not take into account, however, a major change taking place in the way people understand the world to operate, that is, in their worldview. Wuthnow's discussion implies that the internal divisions in various religious groups will result in a rather simple conservative-liberal split. This is not the case in Churches of Christ, nor is it the case in most other bodies suffering separation and fragmentation.

Some readily agree with Wuthnow's assessment, asserting that this liberal-conservative polarization explains what is happening in Churches of Christ. They contend that liberal theology entered our churches a few decades ago and has divided the communion. There may well be some theological liberals who have remained connected with Churches of Christ. Theological liberalism, however, is not our problem today. Most true liberals left our fellowship long ago because of the conservative stance we take on everything from inspiration of Scripture to believer's immersion. Chapter Six is an examination of how the "worldview factor" that is missing in the studies of Wuthnow and other religious sociologists fundamentally changes the nature of this discussion.

Some may want to turn immediately to that material. Taken together, the cycles sketched in this chapter become a complex web that is difficult to sort out. Many answers could be given to the exasperated question, "What is happening?" Some blame generational differences for our problems. Some blame worldliness or secularization, others legalism and narrow dogmatism, and still others lack of convictions and a failure in responsible study of Scripture. All are true to varying degrees.[12]

Churches of Christ are experiencing the same kinds of tensions now dogging groups like the Lutheran Church (Missouri Synod), the Seventh Day Adventists, and especially the Southern Baptist Convention.[13] Many American religious bodies are taking a long, hard look at themselves and using the results of studies to try to understand what is happening.[14] These groups recognize the need to face up to their predicaments, to analyze and understand them and, hopefully with God's help, to do something about them. While the problems of these groups are not necessarily ours, their willingness to confront their difficulties ought to be an example to us. We cannot ignore the problems facing us—they are too serious, and they will not simply go away.

The cycles described in this chapter are primarily sociological models. Sociologists describe; they do not predict.

Yet we would be foolish to dismiss out of hand what social scientists have to teach us. When a group is willing, through the power of God, to understand what is happening and seek biblical, spiritual solutions—perhaps then the cycle can be broken.

Endnotes

[1] See studies like Dean R. Hoge and David A. Roozen, eds., *Understanding Church Growth and Decline*(New York: The Pilgrim Press, 1979); David G. Bromley, ed., *Falling From the Faith: Causes and Consequences of Religious Apostasy* (Newbury Park, CA: Sage Publications, Inc., 1988); and C. Kirk Hadaway, *Church Growth Principles: Separating Fact from Fiction* (Nashville: Broadman Press, 1991).

[2] See Lefferts Loetscher, *The Broadening Church* (Philadelphia: University of Pennsylvania Press, 1957); Ruth B. Bordin, "The Sect to Denomination Process in America: the Freewill Baptist Experience," *Church History* 34 (March 1965):77-94; and John Everett Bungard, "Becoming a Denomination: the Church-Sect Typology and the Stone-Campbell Movement" (Ph.D. Thesis, University of Kansas, 1985).

[3] Wade Clark Roof and William McKinney, *American Mainline Religion: Its Changing Face and Future* (New Brunswick: Rutgers University Press, 1987), 237-8.

[4] Ibid., 109-13.

[5] C. Leonard Allen, Richard T. Hughes, and Michael R. Weed, *The Worldly Church: A Call for Biblical Renewal* (Abilene, TX: ACU Press, 1988).

[6] Renewal groups now exist in all the mainline liberal denominations. See Ronald H. Nash, *Evangelical Renewal in Mainline Churches* (Westchester, IL: Crossway Books, 1987).

[7] David O. Moberg, *The Church as A Social Institution: The Sociology of American Religion*

(Grand Rapids: Baker Book House, 1984), 119-23.

[8] Anthony F. C. Wallace, "Revitalization Movements," *American Anthropologist* 58 (April 1956):264-81. See discussion in Gailyn Van Rheenen, *Communicating Christ in Animistic Contexts* (Grand Rapids: Baker Book House, 1991), 69-75.

[9] Lawrence Cada and others, *Shaping the Coming Age of Religious Life* (New York: Seabury Press, 1979), 51-60. My thanks to David Howard of David Lipscomb University for pointing this material out to me.

[10] Ibid., 76. Another extremely helpful model of the life-cycle of an organization is found in Robert D. Dale's *To Dream Again: How to Help Your Church Come Alive* (Nashville: Broadman Press, 1981). Though directed at individual congregations, many of Dale's insights apply to entire movements, especially his comments about the nostalgia phase of organizational life.

[11] Peggy L. Shriver, "The Paradox of Inclusiveness-that-Divides," *Christian Century* 101(January 21, 1984):194.

[12] The complexities of the situation were reflected in the reaction from different quarters to the material in *The Worldly Church*. Most nervously agreed with the authors' contention that Churches of Christ had bought into society's standards and methods. Yet most went on to criticize the writers' alleged irreverence for the past, use of too many secular sources, implication that we cannot know truth, exaggerations and failure to go far enough in their exposure of our secularism. The critics otherwise disagreed among themselves on many points. See for example Dave Miller, "A Review of the Worldly

Church," *The Restorer* 8 (August 1988):6-12; Alan E. Highers, "A Critique of the Book *The Worldly Church,*" *Gospel Advocate* 130 (April 1, 1988):29-30; Norman L. Parks, "The Worldly Church," *The Examiner* 3 (September 1988):15-16; Art McNeese, "The Christian Bookshelf," *20th Century Christian* 50 (May 1988):32-34.

[13] Roof and McKinney, 234, 238.

[14] Ibid., 148-51. Also D. Newell Williams, ed., *A Case Study of Mainstream Protestantism: The Disciples' Relation to American Culture, 1880-1989* (Grand Rapids: William B. Eerdmans Publishing Company, 1991); Milton J. Coulter, et. al., series *The Presbyterian Presence: The Twentieth-Century Experience* (Louisville: Westminster/John Knox Press, 1990); Bill Leonard, *God's Last and Only Hope: The Fragmentation of the Southern Baptist Convention* (Grand Rapids: William B. Eerdmans Publishing Company, 1990).

Chapter 2

How Others See Us-- The Public Face of
Churches of Christ

O wad some Power the giftie gie us
To see oursels as ithers see us!
It wad frae monie a blunder free us,
An' foolish notion:
What airs in dress an' gait wad lea'e us,
An' ev'n devotion!
—From "To a Louse," by Robert Burns

So ends one of Robert Burns' most famous
poems. Burns had spotted a louse crawling on the
bonnet of an elegantly dressed lady, seated in front of
him in church. All her finery and airs were eclipsed
by the sight of that tiny creature crawling on her head.
The lady, unaware of the impression she was actually
making, became for Burns the classic example of those
unable to see themselves as others see them.

Such situations can develop in groups as well
as individuals. Nations, families, and churches may

be blind to the impressions they make on those outside—impressions that are often very different from the way they see themselves. Some of the material in this chapter is not complimentary. At times it will be obvious that others have misunderstood us—just as we undoubtedly stereotype and misunderstand other groups. The point is that accurate or inaccurate, these are ways others see us.

We cannot blindly accept as valid anything others may think about us. Our ultimate standard is not human perception but God's will and approval. Yet if we can get some true sense of the way outsiders view us, we might be able to understand ourselves a little better and avoid acting in ways that create impressions destructive to our own purposes.

This chapter draws on two categories of material to get a glimpse of how others see us: (1) material about Churches of Christ in the popular media (newspapers, magazines, television, movies), and (2) material from scholarly or semi-scholarly sources (encyclopedias, church history textbooks, journals). This is not an exhaustive examination of all such sources. It is a brief survey of recent materials designed to provide a composite picture of the public face of Churches of Christ.

First, something must be said about perceptions at the personal level. It is not unusual for someone to change a negative opinion of a religious group because of positive contact with individuals from the group. Positive relationships with neighbors, co-workers or fellow PTA members, for example, can create impressions that are very different from formal views of a group and its teachings.

An interesting example of this came out of a

gathering of Southern Baptists and members of Churches of Christ a few years ago. One person from each group was asked to prepare a paper titled "How We See You." The writer of the Baptist paper, a minister from Georgia, polled other Baptist ministers and his own church members to gather impressions of us. He reported, in part, that

> When a group of Baptists were [sic] asked to describe Churches of Christ there was a detectable level of tension as they gave the following responses: "They believe they're the only ones who are saved. . ." "They believe you have to be baptized to go to heaven. . ." "They are very unbending. . ." "It is their way or no way. . ."

This same group of Baptists went on to share additional comments about the Churches of Christ. The more they thought about these churches, the more positive the picture became. "Their church members are warm-hearted. . ." "They are serious about their faith. . ." "They are Bible people like us. . ." "They are family-oriented, mission-minded, Christ-centered folks."

Clearly these Southern Baptists had a corporate picture of Churches of Christ as narrow and rigid. When their thoughts began to center on individuals, however, positive images emerged. The point is, this is not unique; this is what almost always happens! The caution is that the process can also work in the opposite way. Positive impressions can be destroyed by negative encounters.

The perceptions examined below are mostly formal, organizational ones. Those understandings, positive or negative, are the ones people will hold (if they hold any at all) until they have a personal relationship with one of us. How we as individuals relate to others strongly affects the perceptions people have of Churches of Christ. May we be like those early believers described in Acts 2:47 who enjoyed the favor of all the people.

Popular Media Impressions

In cities like Nashville, Tennessee or Abilene and Dallas, Texas—cities with large concentrations of Churches of Christ—newspaper stories often reflect the public's impressions of us. These local news items cover a wide range of matters; some positive, some not. Examples from the last few years include articles on why Churches of Christ do not observe Christmas as holy, a church split in Kentucky over whether members could belong to a Masonic Lodge, a Texas preacher's reasons for leaving Churches of Christ, the firing of a Tennessee minister for "liberalism," and the character of the Nashville Jubilee lectureship.[1]

Attention has been especially focused on the Nashville Jubilee. Since its beginning in 1989, Jubilee has been one of the largest gatherings of members of Churches of Christ in the nation. Jubilee has also drawn criticism from the beginning, and the Nashville papers have featured the controversy, often in front-page articles. The headline for an October 1991 piece, for example, proclaimed "Jubilee Not Traditional Enough for Some. But Target of Right-wing Lambaste Unworried." An opponent of the gathering was quoted as accusing the minister of one of Jubilee's sponsoring congregations of wanting the church to lose its distinctive message and of practicing a type of inter-denominationalism. The minister, in turn, characterized Jubilee's critics as a small and declining right-wing whose loyalties were to "a narrow set of traditions that are neither biblical [n]or Christlike." The following year articles covered a rival lectureship whose speakers charged Jubilee organizers of teaching that worship should be entertainment and that the New Testament was not a pattern.[2]

Another source of local media attention has been disputes over the direction and control of schools. Abilene Christian University has often been the subject of controversy. On Monday of the 1994 ACU Bible Lectureship, a local congregation purchased a full page in the city's newspaper to reprint two articles accusing ACU of departures from the faith.[3] Replies appeared through the rest of the week. One letter characterized the articles as "a frantic, dying gasp," by a shrinking group unhappy with the "refreshing transformation" taking place in Churches of Christ. Another branded it an example of "sectarian hatred" manifested in "a fringe group's desperate effort to control . . ."[4] The conflict even made it onto the local television news.

At the end of the week, Abilene religion editor Roy Jones wrote that, given the current conflicts in American religion generally as well as in Churches of Christ, it was no wonder a conflict management class was one of the most popular of the Lectureship. Jones closed his article by describing the effect this kind of publicity brings to us and others.

> When non-churched persons see any of our organized churches. . . bickering and fighting among ourselves [sic], there's certainly no incentive for them to become involved. In that way we are hurting, not advancing, the cause of Christ. And that's something all of us need desperately to change.[5]

21

On the other hand, positive coverage of Churches of Christ has not been lacking. At the national level, *Christianity Today* reported on our relief efforts in Poland in 1982 and the next year told of aid given by Houston congregations to pay off the million-dollar debt of a failed home for the aged. Frank and Elizabeth Morris, members of the Little River Church of Christ near Hopkinsville, Kentucky, received Associated Press coverage in 1985 when they forgave and befriended the drunken driver who killed their son. The Associated Press in 1993 hailed the Bell Shoals Church in Tampa, Florida, the result of a merger of a black and a white congregation, as a model of racial harmony.[6]

Still another instance of positive coverage is the interview of Larry James, then minister for the Richardson East Church of Christ, by Jane Pauley of "Dateline NBC." The show aired November 17, 1992, featuring the tragic story of Scott Allen, whose wife and children contracted the AIDS virus through blood transfusions. In 1985 James and his congregation opened their church-sponsored day care center to Matt, Allen's HIV-positive son, when no other agency in town would do so.[7]

Perhaps the most widely-known and respected member of Churches of Christ among American evangelicals is Max Lucado, minister of the Oak Hills Church of Christ in San Antonio, Texas. Lucado's writings have touched the hearts of countless thousands. His appearances before a wide variety of religious audiences have summoned criticism from some in Churches of Christ, but have undoubtedly had a positive effect on the way many others see us. The journals *Leadership* and *Preaching* have published

complimentary interviews with Lucado, and his prolific pen continues to inspire readers toward biblical
Christianity and stronger devotion to God.[8]

National media coverage has been especially
focused in four areas. The longest running story is
that of the Crossroads/Boston movement.[9] *Christianity Today* carried major stories on this movement
in 1981 and again in 1988. Under the headline
"Church of Christ Renewal Movement Perplexes
Many," the 1981 article told of the Poway, California
Church of Christ, a "Crossroads" church accused of
cult practices by parents of several members. The
Baptist campus minister at the University of Florida
at Gainesville was quoted as saying, "I could not begin to tell of the damage done to students whom I
have counselled because of the practices of this
church." The article clearly identified the Crossroads
movement as part of Churches of Christ, explaining
that the "Church of Christ has no denominational hierarchy or official spokesman."[10]

In the 1988 article, titled "Boston Church of
Christ Grows Amid Controversy," the group's evangelistic methods and exclusivist attitude were contrasted with the "tradition of freedom of conscience
and congregational autonomy" characteristic of mainstream Churches of Christ.[11] Ironically, the accusation that the Crossroads/Boston movement believed
only those in its ranks would be saved was often the
very charge levelled at mainstream Churches of Christ
in the past.

In a 1992 article, *Time* magazine described the
Boston Church as "one of the world's fastest-grow-
ing and most innovative band of Bible thumpers."
Former Boston member and exit counselor Jeff Davis

commented that the biggest problem with the Boston church is "that the group identifies itself so closely with God that people fear they must forsake God in order to leave it." The article sharply contrasts the Boston Movement with "conventional Churches of Christ, the conservative body of 1.6 million adherents from which [Kip] Mckean and his colleagues broke away."[12] The article clearly implies that mainstream Churches of Christ do not believe that if someone leaves their number they have left God. A March 15,1993 *Newsweek* article on cults mentions the Boston-affiliated Los Angeles Church of Christ, calling it "the fastest growing religious cult in cultic southern California."[13]

Several television documentaries at both the local and national levels have focused on the Boston movement, most pointing to its cultic aspects. A major segment on the International Churches of Christ aired on ABC's "20/20" in October, 1993. Ex-members accused the group of psychological manipulation and mind control, while elder Al Baird denied all such charges. Such publicity has compelled some members of mainstream Churches of Christ to explain, when engaged in public church activities, that they are not connected with the Boston Church of Christ.

The second major event drawing attention to Churches of Christ in the past decade was the case of *Marian Guinn v. the Church of Christ of Collinsville, Oklahoma* in March, 1984. The church publicly withdrew fellowship from Ms. Guinn after she refused to end an affair with a former city mayor. She sued the church for $1.3 million and was awarded $390,000. The case was covered by the Associated Press and United Press International wire services, and articles appeared in newspapers and magazines from the *New York Times* and *Chicago Tribune* to *Time* and *Newsweek*.[14] Memphis minister Garland Elkins even appeared on the Phil Donahue Show to defend the actions of the Collinsville elders.

The attitude of most people seemed to be that the church had no right to tell Ms. Guinn how to live. The American penchant for freedom led most people to assume that such matters are nobody's business but the individual's.

Former Watergate conspirator, Charles Colson, in a 1986 *Christianity Today* column, raised the question of the decision's implications for American churches. Colson contrasted the lack of reaction from the Christian community in the Guinn decision with the actions taken by Christian groups from across the spectrum to defend the rights of Sun Myung Moon in his tax evasion case. Colson contended that the Guinn case was even more important for religious liberty than the Moon litigation. "If the U.S. government seized all of our bank accounts, it could not destroy the church; but if it successfully prevented the church from requiring that its members obey biblical standards, we might as well close our doors."[15]

Colson closed with the question, "Why the passionate defense of Moon, and the embarrassed silence toward the Collinsville elders?" He suggested that it was money, advertising and political connections that made the difference. Could our traditional isolationism have also played a part? Could it be that it simply did not cross the minds of other religious groups that we would want assistance from anyone?

Whether that speculation is true or not, the case received wide publicity for its complexity and implications for the problem of church-state relations. The public perception of Churches of Christ shaped by the Guinn case, however, was generally negative, except among groups like those associated with *Fundamentalist Journal*.[16] Many believed that what the elders at Collinsville did was rigid, authoritarian, and definitely un-American.

The "One Nation Under God" Campaign was the third item drawing national media attention to Churches of Christ. *Christianity Today* noticed the effort in the June 24, 1991 issue. A teaching comic book was to be sent to 100 million American households, the largest mailing in United States history. Hundreds of congregations helped raise the $9 million dollars (down from the original $17 million target) to send this evangelistic piece to the nation.

The July 17, 1991 *Tennessean* reported that most of the comics were sent out around the first of July. Within a little over two weeks the sponsoring congregation, Sycamore Church of Christ in Cookeville, Tennessee, had received 100,000 calls or reply cards from recipients. According to *The Tennessean*, responses were mixed. Some were from atheists, calling Jesus a liar and Christians wimps. Others were from members of other religious groups who lectured them for proselyting, while many were simply lonely.[17]

The campaign drew the attention of *The Door,* a satirical magazine published by Youth Specialties of El Cajon, California. Its September/October 1991 issue awarded the "One Nation Under God" Campaign the "Loser of the Month Award." [See the reprint of the article at the end of this chapter]. They challenged the spending of $9 million to send a comic book to every household in America.

What this nation does not need is 100 million comic books. What it needs is a few hundred thousand people living the Christian life with their neighbors. . . . revival does not need to come to the non-Christians in this country as much as it needs to begin with the Christians who have bought into the pagan belief that the best way to communicate the Gospel is by technology.[18]

Of course there is another side to this, including the many studies and baptisms resulting from the campaign. Nevertheless, *The Door's* portrayal is the impression made on many both within the religious community and outside it. We must consider if there is anything to be learned from this stinging criticism. Does our willingness to support a mass mailing to people somewhere else stem from a desire to avoid the needs of those on our own doorsteps?

The Nashville Jubilee has already been mentioned as receiving considerable attention in the Nashville media. It has in addition been the focus for reporting on Churches of Christ in national journals like *Christianity Today.* Because Jubilee is one of the closest things Churches of Christ have to a national convention, the magazine included it in its reports of summer meetings of religious groups in the September 22, 1989 issue. The report described Churches of Christ as "fiercely autonomous . . . and divid[ing] over such issues as worship style, use of church funds for social-service projects, and policies concerning divorced and remarried believers."

This and the other glimpses of ourselves from the popular media portray some of our strengths but more often reflect the tensions we are now facing. Popular media like newspapers and television tend to focus on the negative. Sensational stories bring attention. How different is the picture painted of us by the more scholarly media?

Scholarly and Semi-Scholarly References

Encyclopedias and dictionaries of American religious groups have been around since the early 1800's. Sometimes the articles are merely edited versions of official statements from the groups themselves. At other times editors spend much time in careful research before writing.

Perhaps the most widely used of these reference books is the *Handbook of Denominations in the United States*, for many years edited by Frank S. Mead. Mead usually relied heavily on information supplied him by the various churches. The first edition of the work, published in 1951, characterized Churches of Christ as a "breach in the ranks of Disciples of Christ." Mead quotes an unnamed source saying that members "do not think of the Churches of Christ as of recent origin, but as established on the first Pentecost after the resurrection and ascension of Christ." He reported that we then had six unofficial publications, that we practice open communion and shun all fraternization with other churches.[19]

The second edition softens the exclusivist emphasis of the first, the writer asserting that we do not claim to be the only Christians or all of Christ's church.[20] The 1965 edition introduces the matter of Christian unity. "There is a distinctive plea for unity at the heart of the Churches of Christ—a unity that is Bible-based." The article goes on to state that "the great scriptural doctrines usually classified as 'conservative' are received in churches of Christ."[21] A frequent theme in the articles is that since we have no institutions with official status that can speak for the entire church, our conformity in ideas and teachings is all the more remarkable.[22] The most noticeable changes in later editions are membership figures, fluctuating between 1.5 and 2.5 million until the 1990 edition which cites the most accurate figure of 1.25 million.

Other works add a variety of perceptions. In *The Religious Bodies of America,* Frederick Mayer described us as "merely a group of independent, autonomous, unattached local congregations" who seemed to represent "the most extreme form of congregationalism among all the churches." Drawing on the work of A. T. DeGroot, Mayer identified five camps within Churches of Christ that were divided over the Sunday school, the college, the one cup, the sequence of the items of worship based on Acts 2:42, and the premillennial coming of Christ.[23]

J. Gordon Melton's *Encyclopedia of American Religions* lists six discernible divisions among Churches of Christ (non-instrumental). After a mainstream centrist group, Melton lists liberal, one-cup, premillennial, non-Sunday school, and conservative (anti-institutional) segments.[24]

We appear as "Churches of Christ (Noninstrumental)" in Arthur Carl Piepkorn's multivolume work on the religious bodies of the United States and Canada. He observes that the religious press in Churches of Christ has "fulfilled many of the functions that denominational organizations supply in other groups." He notes that as many as twenty different kinds of congregations can be found among us, each with its own idea about the proper observance of the "silences of Scripture." He mentions several controversies that had produced divisions, including the paid located preacher, the authority of the local evangelist, whether one local church can take contributions from another local church to support a missionary, and the proper observance of the Lord's Supper. He notes that a majority of us have been sensitive to the demands of Christian social service and support numerous charitable agencies "even while conceding that they are unbiblical."[25]

Leo Rosten, editor of *Religions of America*, allows Churches of Christ only a quick mention in the section on the Disciples of Christ, chiefly to avoid any confusion of the groups.[26] Sociologist David Moberg in *The Church as a Social Institution* lists Churches of Christ as a legalistic or objectivist sect. Such groups, Moberg says,

> stress certain definite, performable rules, rituals, observances, or objects, or the denial or rejection of some practice, as essential to true religion. They often consider themselves to be the 'true church' or the restorers of Biblical Christianity.[27]

Histories of American religion have generally viewed Churches of Christ as a conservative reactionary split from the Disciples. In the award-winning *A Religious History of the American People*, Sidney Ahlstrom asserted that despite our radical congregationalism, we had been able to proselytize and adapt so well that he believed we were then (1972) "the most dynamic large denomination in the South, and [had] developed considerable strength in other sections and abroad."[28] He also remarked that our internal controversies involved points that had no important place in the larger history of Christianity, comprehensible only to other restorationists.

In the most recent edition of Edwin Gaustad's *A Religious History of America,* he points to our "rigid congregational polity" that kept us out of participation in any activity with other religious bodies and prevented development of denominational headquarters, national programs, institutions and boards. He also points out that our centers of strength are in Tennessee, Arkansas and Texas.[29]

A widely used textbook is Winthrop Hudson's *Religion in America.* In Hudson's work we get only part of a footnote that describes us as the "rigidly biblistic wing of the Disciples—the Churches of Christ of the Middle South."[30] In the third (1981) edition an added mention asserts that the membership figures we then claimed were undoubtedly inaccurate.[31] A recent addition to the list of American religious histories, Mark Noll's *A History of Christianity in the United States and Canada,* includes us in a couple of lists, and says that we (along with Disciples) parallel the Methodists in regional strength with a plurality in the upper South and lower Midwest.[32]

Martin Marty, dean of American church historians, devotes four pages to Disciples in volume one of his *Modern American Religion.* We are described as "a separate movement off to the right," a group of "'digressive' churches in a denomination turning 'progressive.'"[33]

While we do not figure prominently in most histories of American religion, an entire volume has been devoted to Churches of Christ in the new Greenwood Press series on American churches. This is in addition to a volume on the Christian Church

(Disciples of Christ). These books are part of a major reference work on American religious groups, continuing the tradition of the *American Church History* series published almost one hundred years ago. The very fact that we have been included is evidence of the importance the scholarly community has come to give us in recent years.

Another entire volume was devoted to the Restoration Movement by the Roman Catholic Glenmary Research Center in Atlanta. The book was originally designed to explain Churches of Christ to Catholics, and author Richard Tristano makes a number of interesting observations about us. At one point he asserts that conservative Roman Catholics and members of Churches of Christ have much in common, particularly in their theology of baptism and the church.[34]

At the 1991 Christian Scholars Conference, an observer whose responsibility it is to keep up with "non-ecumenical" groups, was impressed with our "special heritage of seeking so seriously to follow Christ." She commented on the remarkable fellowship among the participants, "a tribute to the power of journals, lectures, and the colleges to hold these Christians in community effectively, despite congregational autonomy, and to the power of Christian affection."

On the other hand she reported some disturbing things, concluding that much of our current turmoil was due, as much as anything else, to "self-imposed isolation interpreted as fidelity." Taking her cue from statements heard at the conference, she told the following fable.

> Human beings should love each other and overcome their tribalism. We think that what would help is to have everyone drop their last names, which only bespeak a clannish spirit, and become just Jane Humanbeing and John Humanbeing. People who have not done this are clannish so we will have nothing to do with them. The [problem] is that nobody else in the world knows they have been written off by the "human-beings-only-but-not-the-only-human-beings" movement. So the question is, how effective a witness is that? . . . just who is being clannish?[35]

Such reactions by people who have studied us carefully and sympathetically should give us considerable food for thought.

Perhaps best placed in its own category is a class of extremely anti-Restoration literature characterized by the writings of independent Baptist Bob L. Ross. A prolific writer and debater, Ross has published at least four books and numerous tracts giving his perceptions of Churches of Christ. In *Campbellites, Cow Bells, Rosary Beads and Snake Handling,* Ross asserts that the main teachings of Churches of Christ are

> denials of Bible doctrine and practice which they observe in other professing Christian groups. They are on a "mission" of "accreditation by discreditation;" that is, they "prove" they are "right" by "proving" every other group to be "wrong."

Ross goes on to accuse us of making the silence of Scripture into a great doctrinal heresy. By the time we have finished reasoning and inferring from Scripture, he contends, we "have constructed a veritable maze of confusion from which there is no escape apart from the grace of God."[36] Ross has waged his "anti-Campbellite" campaign for over thirty years.

One cannot help but wonder what sort of negative experience Ross had with some of us early in his life.

Finally, how are we regarded in histories of the Restoration Movement written by scholars in the other "branches" of the Movement? The two most recent examples of these histories are *Journey in Faith: A History of the Christian Church (Disciples of Christ)* by Lester G. McAllister and William E. Tucker, and *In Search of Christian Unity: A History of the Restoration Movement,* by Henry Webb. McAllister and Tucker mention that Churches of Christ have a common heritage with the Disciples, but that otherwise we are unrelated. They discuss the division of the late 1800's, but we receive no notice beyond that.[37]

Henry Webb of the conservative Christian Churches devotes an entire chapter of his book to the prospects of Churches of Christ for the twenty-first century. He focuses heavily on our avoidance of instrumental music in worship and wonders if our move up the economic and cultural ladder in recent decades might bring us to question the central nature we have given the instrument matter. He also remarks that the role of women is more restricted in Churches of Christ than in either Disciples or Christian Churches. Our isolation from all other religious groups and our predominantly Southern character are characteristics he believes stand out, and he observes that our college lectureships serve much the same function that the conventions serve for the Christian Churches.

Webb closes the chapter by contrasting our emphasis on doctrinal correctness and conformity to a New Testament pattern with the widespread interest among religious people in understanding the presence

and work of the Holy Spirit. Our most serious challenge, he suggests, is to be able to "address mean-
ingfully the emotional emptiness and personal frustra-
tions of contemporary society while retaining [our]
doctrinal emphasis. . ."[38]

Assessment: How Others See Us

What then is the picture painted of Churches
of Christ by this array of descriptions? On the one
hand we appear to many as sectarian exclusivists,
combative, divisive, and legalistic, with doctrinal positions that are incomprehensible to most of our neighbors. We seem to some to be isolated, naive,
ahistorical restorationists with tendencies toward
oppressive control of members' lives, refusing relations of any kind with other religious groups.

On the other hand, we are known for our tradition of freedom of conscience and fierce congregational autonomy, being held together by an amazing
informal consensus and Christian affection. We are
counter-cultural, upholding high moral standards, yet
socially sensitive. We are evangelistic, pressing for a
biblical Christian unity.

Which is the correct picture? The answer
is both. . . and neither. We are not perfect. Neither
are we hopeless. We must put both criticism and praise
into the proper context, evaluating them in light of
God's Word. The truth is, most people have no impression of Churches of Christ at all. If in our personal encounters we can increasingly manifest the fruit
of the Spirit described in Galatians 5, we have the
opportunity to create the kind of public face we should
want, above all else, to have.

So in everything, do to others what you would have them do to you, for this sums up the Law and the Prophets.

—Matthew 7:12

If it is possible, as far as it depends on you, live at peace with everyone.

—Romans 12:17

If you keep on biting and devouring each other, watch out or you will be destroyed by each other. . . But the fruit of the Spirit is love, joy, peace, patience, kindness, goodness, faithfulness, gentleness and self-control.

—Galatians 5:15, 22-23

Endnotes

[1] Ray Waddle, "No Decked Halls: Most Churches of Christ Don't Observe Christmas as Holy," *The Tennessean* (December 25, 1990):1A-2A; Ray Waddle, "Church of Christ Minister Runs Masons Out of Congregation," *The Tennessean* (February 9, 1992):1A-2A; Frances Meeker, "Hendersonville Church Ends 'Liberal' Service of Minister," *Nashville Banner* (August 14, 1991):B-4; Daniel Cattau, "Preacher Follows Own Conscience, Starts Church," *The Dallas Morning News* (September 12, 1992):38A; Ray Waddle, "Church of Christ Dilemma: Stay with Basics, Change with Society?" *The Tennessean* (July 17, 1991):1A-2A; Frances Meeker, "Jubilee Unites Church's Family," *Nashville Banner* (July 4, 1991):B-1.

[2] Francis Meeker, "Jubilee Not Traditional Enough for Some," *The Nashville Banner* (October 14, 1991):B1, B4; Ray Waddle, "Churches' Lectures Counter 'Heretical' Jubilee Teachings," *The Tennessean* (September 5, 1992):1B-2B; Francis Meeker, "Jubilee Celebration Makes Churches of Christ a House Divided," *The Nashville Banner* (July 5, 1994): A1-A2

[3] "An Open Letter to Abilene Christian University," and "An Open Letter to Royce Money," *Abilene Reporter-News* (February 21, 1994):7A.

[4] Mike Cope, "A Last Gasp," *Abilene Reporter-News* (February 22, 1994):6A; Darryl Tippens, "Vicious Hatred Helps No One," *Abilene Reporter-News* (February 23, 1994):8A.

[5] Roy A. Jones II, "'Conflict Management' a Popular Lectureship Class," *Abilene Reporter-News* (February 26, 1994):1E.

[6] Harry Genet, "Churches Respond to a Hungry Poland," *Christianity Today* 26(February 2, 1982):46-47; "North American Scene," *Christianity Today* 27(March 4, 1983):69; David McCormick, "Couple 'Adopts' Son's Killer: Man Speaks for MADD," *Christian Chronicle* 42(August 1985):6; *Baltimore Sun* (January 18, 1993):6A, cited in Gary Pearson, "From *True Grit* to *Molly Ivans Can't Say That, Can She?* A Survey of Outside Perspectives on Churches of Christ," presented at the Pepperdine Lectures, April 28, 1993. Special thanks are due Pearson for sharing his paper which enhanced this chapter at several points.

[7] Reuters transcript report, "Dateline NBC," November 17, 1992, 14.

[8] Marshall Shelley and Brian Larson, "The

Applause of Heaven and Earth: An Interview with Max Lucado," *Leadership* 13 (Summer 1992): 14-22; Michael Duduit, "Preaching the Empty Tomb: An Interview with Max Lucado," *Preaching* 8 (March/April 1993): 4-11.

[9]" Crossroads" was the early name of the movement because it was centered in the campus ministry of the Crossroads Church of Christ in Gainesville, Florida. It was later called the Boston Movement because of the location of chief leaders, particularly Kip McKean, in that city. The movement is now called the International Churches of Christ, headquartered in Los Angeles. Also called Discipling Ministries or Multiplying Ministries. See Flavil R. Yeakley, Jr., *The Discipling Dilemma* (Nashville: Gospel Advocate Co., 1988) and Robert H. Nelson, *Understanding the Crossroads Controversy* (Fort Worth: Star Bible Publications, Inc., 1985).

[10] Lloyd Billingsley, "A Church of Christ Renewal Movement Perplexes Many," *Christianity Today* 25 (November 20, 1981):54.

[11] Carlene B. Hill, "Boston Church of Christ Grows Amid Controversy," *Christianity Today* 32 (February 19, 1988):53.

[12] Richard N. Ostling, "Keepers of the Flock," *Time* 142 (May 18, 1992):62.

[13] Kenneth L. Woodward, "Cultic America: A Tower of Babel," *Newsweek* 121(March 15, 1993):61.

[14] See Merlin R. Mann, "A Content Analysis of Print Media Reporting of the Collinsville, Okla., Church of Christ Privacy Case," (M.A. thesis, Abilene Christian University, 1986).

[15] Charles Colson, "Friends of Religious Liberty: Why the Embarrassing Silence?" *Christianity*

Today 30 (April 18, 1986):56.

[16] See for example "Woman Wins $390,000 Lawsuit against Church," *Fundamentalist Journal* 3 (June 1984):64; and Ralph D. Mawdsley, "The Modus Operandi of Church Discipline," *Fundamentalist Journal* 3 (November 1984):22-24.

[17] Ray Waddle, "Cookeville Church Gets Positive, Negative Response to Mailing," *The Tennessean* (July 17, 1991):2A.

[18] "Loser of the Month," *The Door* (September/October 1991):32.

[19] Frank S. Mead, *Handbook of Denominations in the United States* (Nashville: Abingdon Press, 1951), 59-60.

[20] Ibid., 2nd ed. (1956), 68-69.

[21] Ibid., 4th ed. (1965), 87-89.

[22] Ibid., 6th ed.(1975), 106-9.

[23] Frederick Emanuel Mayer, *The Religious Bodies of America* (St. Louis: Concordia Publishing House, 1956), 384-5.

[24] J. Gordon Melton, *Encyclopedia of American Religions* vol. 1 (Wilmington, North Carolina: McGrath Publishing Co., 1978), 405-8.

[25] Arthur Carl Piepkorn, *Profiles in Belief: The Religious Bodies of the United States and Canada,* vol. II, *Protestant Denominations* (New York: Harper and Row, 1977), 636-41.

[26] Leo Rosten, *Religions of America* (New York: Simon and Schuster, 1975), 84-85.

[27] David Moberg, *The Church as a Social Institution* (Grand Rapids: Baker Book House, 1984), 91.

[28] Sidney Ahlstrom, *A Religious History of the American People* (New Haven: Yale University Press, 1972), 822-3.

[29] Edwin Gaustad, *A Religious History of America* (San Francisco: Harper & Row, 1990), 258-9.

[30] Winthrop S. Hudson, *Religion in America* (New York: Scribner, 1965), 277.

[31] Ibid., 3rd ed., 454.

[32] Mark A. Noll, *A History of Christianity in the United States and Canada* (Grand Rapids: Eerdmans, 1992), 473.

[33] Martin E. Marty, *Modern American Religion,* vol. 1, *The Irony of It All: 1893-1919* (Chicago: The University of Chicago Press, 1986), 162-3.

[34] Richard M. Tristano, *The Origins of the Restoration Movement: An Intellectual History* (Atlanta: Glenmary Research Center, 1988), 11.

[35] Elizabeth H. Mellen, [Report on the Eleventh Annual Christian Scholars Conference], Graymoor Ecumenical and Interreligious Institute, March, 1994, 7.

[36] Bob L. Ross, *Campbellites, Cow Bells, Rosary Beads and Snake Handling* (Pasadena, Texas: Pilgrim Publications, 1994), 7, 8. See also *Campbellism: Its History and Heresies* (Pasadena, Texas: Pilgrim Publications, 1962), and *Acts 2:38 and Baptismal Regeneration* (Pasadena, Texas: Pilgrim Publications, 1976).

[37] Lester G. McAllister and William E. Tucker, *Journey in Faith: A History of the Christian Church (Disciples of Christ)* (St. Louis: The Bethany Press, 1975), 29.

[38] Henry E. Webb, *In Search of Christian Unity: A History of the Restoration Movement* (Cincinnati: Standard Publishing, 1990), 407-18.

LOSER OF THE MONTH

Nine million dollars for 100 million comic books.

Please, say it isn't true.

Why is the Church so willing to spend millions on the latest advertising scheme and so *un*willing to spend its money on the things that matter?

It is not enough to say that the people involved with this scheme are well-meaning. That's the trouble. There is so much waste rendered by well-meaning people in the Church that we have all kept quiet.

It is time to quit being quiet. This $9 million is a mistake. A big mistake. The One Nation Under God campaign is a nine million dollar Green

Weenie if we've ever seen one. What this nation does *not* need is 100 million comic books. What it *needs* is a few hundred thousand people living the Christian life with their neighbors. *Then* we would see revival. To be quite honest, every time we see something like this we realize that revival does not need to come to the *non*-Christians in this country as much as it needs to begin with the Christians who have bought into the pagan belief that the best way to communicate the Gospel is by technology.

So, to Horace Burks and the rest of the misguided supporters of this scheme, we sadly present the Loser of the Month Award.

Here's the plan.
We need $9 million dollars now. You might have to mortgage home, sell your stamp collection hatever it takes to reach that
  Trust us. The need is urgent. tever it takes, we need the $9 on.
Why?
We want to send an eight-page c book to 100 million Ameri- iomes.
Jh ... you're kidding, right?
Ve are, yes, but Horace Burks camore Church of Christ .00 other Churches of Christ ot kidding. At the time of rinting, almost all of the $9 on had been raised and 60 on of the comic books had dy been mailed by a onaire named Horace s and his home church okeville, TN, the nore Church of Christ.

Reprinted with permission from *The Door* magazine (issue #119), Box 530, Yreka, California 96097

41

Will the Cycle be Unbroken?

Chapter 3

How We See Ourselves

Humans are prone to self-deception. Too often we either think of ourselves more highly than we ought or become overly self-critical. Mentally healthy people reevaluate their self-understanding frequently in light of both the perceptions of others (positive and negative) and the ideal person they want to be.

The same is true of organizations. We have seen a kaleidoscope of outsiders' impressions of us. Now we must deal with how we understand ourselves. It should come as no surprise that, just as there was no single view of Churches of Christ from the outside, there is no single internal understanding either.[1]

Our Concept of the Church

How we see ourselves depends finally on how we understand the church. Stated plainly, how do we view the relationship of the identifiable group known as Churches of Christ to God's universal church?

One strongly held view is that the body known as Churches of Christ is equivalent to the universal church. One of the most famous statements of that position was made by David Edwin Harrell, Jr., in his 1966 Reed Lecture at the Disciples of Christ Historical Society. Asked to speak on the relation of "his group" to the church universal, Harrell frankly stated, "From my theological point of view, the group to which I belong *is* the church universal."[2]

The non-institutional Churches of Christ of which Harrell is a member perhaps embody that position more uniformly than mainstream congregations.[3] Yet the sentiment is by no means confined to that part of the movement. A common approach among those who hold this view is to create headings such as "Why the church of Christ is Not a Denomination" or "Why I Am a Member of the church of Christ,"[4] and then list New Testament passages that speak of Christ's universal body. If understood in the biblical sense, the authors' points are irrefutable. Christ's universal church is not a denomination or a sect. The authors often make it quite clear, however, that they are talking about the visible fellowship of congregations known exclusively as Churches of Christ.

> From the perspective of the world, the church of Christ is a denomination. They see a group that is independent from other groups, so they assume it is merely another of the groups in the denominational system. It is true, of course, that the church of Christ is a separate people; but the church of Christ is not a division of the body of Christ. **It is the body of Christ.** Those who are uninformed may not understand this, and are in need of teaching and study.[5]

Those holding this view refuse to fellowship or acknowledge the true Christian identity of any but those churches of like heritage and practice identified as Churches of Christ.[6]

This view has been central to our message in the twentieth century and is reflected in our language. When we speak of "the Lord's Church," we mean only our congregations. "The New Testament church" means the churches produced by our efforts at restoration. Even when we simply say "the church," we know precisely what the term refers to. The fragmentation in Churches of Christ in recent years has pushed some to use the term "faithful churches of Christ" or "true churches of Christ" to designate those acceptable to the user.[7] "The Old Paths," "New Testament Christianity," "the pattern"—all are composed of perfectly understandable English words, but we use these phrases in a way only the initiated can understand. They form part of our "dialect" and reflect a particular understanding of the church.

On the other hand, the view that Churches of Christ constitute a movement within the universal church is epitomized by the early Restoration slogan "Not the only Christians, but Christians only." The churches formed by the efforts of the Campbells, Stone, Scott and countless others did not claim to contain all Christians. Rather, they wanted all Christians to drop tests of fellowship based on denominational creeds and structures and be simply Christians. Those who still hold to this concept point out that Christ's universal church is over nineteen hundred years old and encompasses untold millions of believers, alive and dead, who had no knowledge of nor connection with the American-born Churches of Christ.[8] The

45

statement of purpose for *Wineskins* magazine expresses this understanding:

> Our background and commitment is to the Church of Christ that was born of the American Restoration Movement. Our goal is to move that group closer to the church of Christ revealed in Scripture.

The *Wineskins* statement also points to a peculiarity in conveying our concept of the church—spelling! Many of us have insisted on using the lowercase "c," as in "church of Christ" or "churches of Christ," to indicate that the phrase is not a proper name, but a simple description: this church belongs to Christ. As G. C. Brewer pointed out, however, this mode of thought can easily slip into gross sectarianism.

> Some unthinking brethren seem to hold that to spell church with a small "c" avoids making a title or proper name of the phrase 'church of Christ.' This is laughable. When the sense is plainly a designation—a telling of "what" church is intended—then the phrase is used as a proper name, and thus the scriptures are violated [by using a scriptural phrase for all the saved to apply to only a portion], and to use a small initial letter in a proper name is to violate the laws of grammar. So, brother, you are both unscriptural and ungrammatical.[9]

Complications in Our Understandings

Within these two broad views of the church are several complications to our understanding that we must deal with. The first has to do with vocabulary; specifically, the terms "sect" and "denomination." The Stone-Campbell Restoration Movement began with an inherent antagonism toward sectarianism and denominationalism—terms often used interchangeably to designate divisive structures.

Followers of Christ are to be united. Anything dividing believers is evil. The early Restoration leaders did not set out to create a new denomination. Instead, they challenged Christians in all the "sects" to renounce denominational creeds and structures as tests of fellowship and be simply Christians.

No one who believes the New Testament can honestly contend that division among Christians is what Christ wanted (John 17:20-23). Certainly it must be possible in some sense to be simply a Christian, unbound by creedal formulas and denominational structures. Yet the realities of this world quickly and easily subvert the concept of undenominational or nonsectarian Christianity. As a result, Churches of Christ are a separate, identifiable religious body. If we use the term in this sense, we constitute a denomination.

Does such an admission mean that we have sold out our anti-denominational heritage? Some would answer an emphatic "yes." They would assert that if we equate the Churches of Christ with the universal church we must reject any acknowledgment of denominational status, because Christ's universal church is not a denomination. Others readily acknowledge that at the social, cultural and historical level we, like all others, cannot avoid thinking of ourselves and being thought of as a separate group.

Yet people who refuse to allow creeds (written or unwritten) and structures (formal or informal) to prevent them from recognizing and fellowshipping all who seek to follow Christ and do God's will, have in some sense become undenominational and nonsectarian. Such a stance is certainly in line with that taken by the early leaders of the Restoration Movement. This perspective is compatible with the notion that there is always more to learn and that fellow travelers can aid one another in the movement toward God.

Sociologists of religion would say that Churches of Christ are in the process of moving from a sect to a denomination, from a position against society to being part of society. Perhaps that is undeniable at the sociological level. But the question keeps coming back: is it possible to understand ourselves as truly non-sectarian and undenominational? A fundamental problem in answering this is that those who hold different concepts of the church also understand the terms "sectarian" and "denominational" in completely opposite ways.

Those who see Churches of Christ exclusively as the universal church view all who believe there are persons saved by Christ outside our borders, as sectarians. The contention that the Churches of Christ (usually written "churches of Christ" or "church of Christ") constitute a sect or denomination is inconceivable to them. They contend that Christ's church is not a denomination, but consists of all the saved; it is the blood-bought bride. To assert that there are true Christians in other groups, therefore, is to endorse sectarianism, denominationalism, and division.[10]

On the other hand, to those who see Churches of Christ as a body of people dedicated to following Christ, but not the only ones legitimately making that effort, the above viewpoint appears to be the ultimate example of sectarianism. This second group agrees wholeheartedly that Christ's church encompasses all the saved and that it is not a denomination. They insist, however, that Christ's church is not confined to one visible, historically-bound body named Churches of Christ. Both sides condemn sectarianism, but each holds a radically different concept of what it is.

This last view of the church is by no means a recent phenomenon. There have always been respected voices in Churches of Christ who have insisted that neither biblical Christianity nor our immediate heritage were exclusive in nature. Doctrinally conservative and loyal to Churches of Christ, these voices have insisted that the bounds of God's family are not confined to our fellowship. People like G. C. Brewer (d. 1956) and Monroe Hawley have insisted that we cannot and must not equate our visible fellowship of Churches of Christ, as great and noble as it is, with the universal church.

> Any institution that does not include all of God's children cannot be the church of God. Even if such an institution is composed entirely of Christians, contains only Christians, and yet does not contain all Christians, it cannot be the church of God. . . .To apply the terms *the church,* or the church of God or the church of Christ to any limited number of Christians is to sectarianize these scriptural phrases. . . We have, in spite of ourselves, become a sect whose special purpose is to contend against sectarianism.[11]

> The issue is not whether a group of disciples has the right to claim to be Christians only. Rather, it is whether those who are "Christians only" can justifiably profess to be the only Christians and that all others are thereby outside the borders of the kingdom of God.
> The boundaries of the kingdom encompass all who have been born into the divine family . . . Only God can expunge their names from the book of life. For us to exclude them because we perceive some error in their thinking or practice is to be guilty of sectarian judgmentalism.[12]

The Restoration of the Church

A second factor we must consider in

evaluating our understanding of the church is our heritage of restorationism. Our perception of the church has always been closely linked to the matter of restoring New Testament Christianity. The leaders of the Stone-Campbell Movement understood restoration of the New Testament church as the necessary step that would lead to the unity of Christians and the conversion of the world.[13] For part of the movement, restoration—particularly of correct doctrine and form—became the chief end. Some believe that the New Testament church was restored at some point in the past through the efforts that came from the American Restoration Movement. The Churches of Christ are, they believe, the restored New Testament church. The job now is to be vigilant against any deviation from that completed restoration. "The church was restored and continues to maintain its distinctiveness and exclusiveness only by powerful and plain preaching and defense of the truth."[14]

Others, still very conservative in belief, are less absolute in their claims for perfect restoration. One idea these present is that, though we have recovered correct doctrine and worship practices, we are still lacking in areas such as the evangelistic zeal and church discipline that characterized the early church.[15] Another concept often expressed in the past is that while we might not be perfect, we are closer to the ideal than anyone else. Batsell Barrett Baxter, for example, urged,

> "Take the New Testament as the blueprint or pattern and then come across the centuries to our own day. Then find the church that is most like the pattern."[16]

That church, of course, would be the Churches of Christ.

At the other end of the spectrum are voices who emphasize that restoration is a never-ending process—a quest that will always occupy sincere Christians, both collectively and individually. For these people, the goal is continual study and learning, openness to the Word, self-examination and correction in light of the Word, and a continual, faithful movement toward what God would have us be. Because we are imperfect humans, they insist, the process never ends.[17]

The implications of holding one or another of these views are great. If we believe we have completely restored true Christianity, we must reject the possibility of the existence of true Christians who hold beliefs and practices that differ from ours. The strong tendency is to condemn anyone seeking to follow Christ from outside our communion and any inside who deviate from our norms. If, on the other hand, we accept the view that we are a body of imperfect humans seeking truth and trying to honor Christ in our lives, we must admit that others, though starting at different places, may genuinely be trying to do the same in the midst of their own imperfections.

The matter becomes even more complicated when some among us deny they have any connection with the American Restoration Movement. "We base our religious beliefs and practices solely on the clear teachings of the New Testament," they argue. Holders of this assumption would state that all honest people in every age can read and understand the New Testament correctly and alike. Therefore, those who have done so today do not owe their understandings to any historical movement or person. They declare that they have simply gone to the source of authority, the Bible, and reproduced New Testament Christianity in its original form. In other words, they believe they would have produced the church in precisely its current condition even if there had never been a Barton W. Stone or an Alexander Campbell or an American Restoration Movement. Extreme proponents of this idea deny that we even have an American Restoration heritage.

> In the guest editorial [What Is Good About the Church] references were repeatedly made to a "Restoration Movement," "our movement," "the restoration tradition," etc. In more than 40 years of preaching form [sic] the Bible this language is puzzling to me. . . We do not have "our movement;" Jesus Christ has his Body, his Church, his Family. We strive to be a part of that fellowship, avoiding any sectarian movements or memberships.[18]

Others insist that while our American Restoration history may be important, our real heritage is not in the nineteenth century A.D., but in the first.[19]

The fact is, one *cannot* be simply a member of an ethereal "church at large" that has no human component. That idea is both dangerous and unscriptural. There is no such thing as a detached, historyless, non-human church. The church is of divine origin, yet it is by necessity and very definition composed of human beings—human beings with a history and culture that cannot be avoided.

Churches of Christ have a history and culture that we cannot escape. We must, within the bounds of our history and heritage, seek to come to God—and that is true for everyone! In this sense, the church is unavoidably a "cultural church."[20]

How We See Our Current Situation

For well over a decade, a growing number of writers, preachers and other thought-shapers have maintained that Churches of Christ are experiencing an "identity crisis." This psychological term refers to a state in which persons or institutions have lost a clear concept of their defining attributes. Perhaps, having lived isolated for so long in their own subculture or having mindlessly moved along with the larger culture, they find themselves caught off-guard by change. Old ways of thinking and doing are no longer appropriate or acceptable. Not having a clear picture of whom they really are, and having based their identity on culturally-defined externals that have begun to change radically, a crisis occurs.

No one can deny that Churches of Christ are in a period of transition and tension. The resulting anxiety only serves to aggravate the differences of perception discussed above. Some are pessimistic about our future, asserting that Churches of Christ seem bent on self-destruction.

> Everywhere one looks congregations are in trouble—members are leaving, preachers are being fired, elders face tremendous stress, young people are discouraged, contributions are down.[21]
> I fear that there are some dark clouds gathering on the brotherhood's horizon.[22]

Others, even from very different perspectives, are optimistic about the future.

> There are signs in many places that brethren are reversing this trend [toward liberalism], standing up to the preachers and professors who have led them down the primrose path, and returning once again to a strong emphasis on the fundamentals.[23]

> We are presently witnessing the emergence of many congregations from the isolationism of the past. These congregations are equipping themselves to meet the problems of our present world, not those of fifty years ago. I believe we are presently witnessing a greater spirituality among our people. Today there is a greater willingness to examine biblical truths anew rather than to simply defend the status quo.[24]

Some believe that our current tensions are primarily generational. It is true that younger generations are usually more open to change, and the acceptance of even appropriate changes often seems to condemn the teachings and methods of earlier generations. Yet, deciding that gospel meetings no longer fit a congregation's evangelistic program, for example, does not imply that holding gospel meetings is an inherently bad method. None should assume that change itself is a denunciation of the methods of older generations.

Certainly, generational conflicts are one significant part of our present crisis. It may be that the growth of youth programs in the 1950's and following years tended to isolate young people from the thinking of their elders. Such conflicts, however, are characteristic of every age. Perhaps our present conflicts have been made worse by the rapid pace and intensity of changes in our culture and within the church. And yet, all ages can be found in every position across our spectrum. Generational conflict alone is simply not a sufficient explanation for what is happening to us now.

In the minds of some, our problems are the result of a new movement, often viewed as a conspiracy, that is seen as a conscious effort to change long-held beliefs and practices in Churches of Christ. A speaker at the 1990 Freed-Hardeman University Lectures urged his audience not to "sell out the church of the Lord."[25] One editor, in a letter to the readers of his paper, characterized our present situation as "a life and death struggle for gospel truth against . . . organized compromisings. . ." He urged readers to join him in "defending the true gospel against those who would destroy it among the true churches of Christ."[26]

Lack of respect for Scripture is the chief accusation leveled against those seen as part of this "new movement." It is alleged that in an effort to be conformed to this world, such people are leaving clear scriptural teachings concerning matters such as the role of women in the church, the use of instrumental music in worship, the New Testament as a pattern for the church, the essential nature of immersion, and opposition to denominations. Their opponents maintain that they have succumbed to the moral laxity and secularism rampant in today's society. Alarm has been expressed in many quarters. In at least two articles in the February 1992 issue of the *Gospel Advocate,* the writers called for increased vigilance in detecting and documenting instances of apostasy or the teaching of error.[27]

Several, in fact, insist that our current situation is identical to that of the 1890's, when theological liberals among Christian Churches were rejecting fundamental biblical truths. [See an evaluation of this idea in Chapter Six.] Today's situation is just as clear, they contend. There is no room for wavering, and everyone must get on the right side.

Interestingly, the anti-institutional proponents of the 1950's and 1960's said the same thing. They believed that the Herald of Truth and church-supported orphan's homes as they were structured were unscriptural human institutions, like the missionary society of the 1800's. Not surprisingly, leaders in the anti-institutional churches are increasingly calling for conservatives in "liberal" mainstream Churches of Christ to come over to them, and with some success.[28]

Naturally those who see a new and dangerous movement in the church feel compelled to take a combative stance. Calls to take sides in the struggle increased in the mid-1980's. The statements below are typical of these battle cries:

> The church is going through radical change because of radical liberalism; therefore we must become all the more militant in our stand for truth and right. Our enemies are powerful and deep-seated.[29]
> There is NOW a time to pick sides, cross the line, and follow our war leader. . . Brethren, let us take up the sword of the Spirit and let the world and false brethren hear the dreadful sound of it unsheathing. Brethren, the campaign is on! The enemy is mobilized and their campfires alight the sky! Our war King calls us to close quarters saying, Whosoever cometh not forth . . . so shall it be done eternally unto him.[30]

Often those who take such a militant position toward the rest of their brothers and sisters see themselves as a faithful remnant—few in number, yet destined to triumph in the end.

Over against these cries for open warfare are a number of other voices. In a 1977 *Firm Foundation* article, Reuel Lemmons wrote that Churches of Christ had expended more effort in making and keeping the church "pure" than in saving souls. Furthermore, he said, most of the purifying efforts were directed toward making churches conform to some brother's hobby. Lemmons asserted that Churches of Christ were in need of a painful self-examination of where we are and where we are going. He stated that we have been divided through the years by dictators who were able to gain control of part of the church. Our only hope of survival, he insisted, lay in our willingness to constantly reassess our position. "Any time we become a closed system, bent on defending the faith by purging the heretics, rather than an eager people hungry for truth, we doom ourselves."[31]

Lemmons was right. Yet the maxim must be applied across the board. Every individual, congregation, group or faction must be willing to make this painful self-examination, measuring itself against scriptural authority. "When we reach the place where we think we have arrived, and have need of nothing, we have, in reality, reached the other end of the line."[32] For any movement to survive and continue to be vital, it must constantly be renewed. Without renewal the options are eventually reduced to stagnation and death on one hand, or revolution on the other.

It is important for Christians to understand who our enemy really is. Sisters and brothers who use different teaching methods, or who make a controversial judgment call, or who structure worship differently from the traditional formats, but who are not guilty of moral sin or clear doctrinal error are not enemies of the cross. Our enemy is the Devil (1 Peter 5:8). Satan delights in getting Christians to bite and devour one another, for he knows that then they will destroy each other, handing him the victory (Galatians

5:15). Those characterized by the fruit of the Spirit will not be engaged in discord, jealousy, selfishness and dissensions. Those ruled by the sinful nature will.

Churches of Christ face some serious problems. We are more secularized and materialistic than many of us have been willing to admit.[33] Too often we have focused energies away from serious Bible study. But even when we have put great emphasis on biblical knowledge, we may have "neglected the weightier things; love, justice, and mercy" (Matthew 23:23).[34]

The tendency in times of tension and change is to polarize, to choose up sides. But however we may label the current opposing forces, we have no obligation to take sides in these fights. Our obligation is to fear God and keep his commandments. Our sole responsibility is, with the help of God, to follow Jesus Christ as he directs in his Word. That pursuit will automatically place us against certain ideas and practices—not because we have chosen sides in a human fight, but because we have a commitment to Christ. In honoring that commitment, we must avoid the extremes that plague human efforts. We need to be more concerned with being part of God's kingdom than being on the "right side" in a fight.[35]

The Uniqueness of Churches of Christ

To many, the changes taking place in Churches of Christ threaten to destroy our uniqueness. These believe if we are not unique, we have no right to continued existence.

> Unless the church of Christ is different from all other religious institutions it has no lawful right to exist as a separate body. Unless these differences are

necessary, and unless they can be found collected in no other one body, we likewise have no right to exist.[36]

The problem is embedded in the assertion of the necessity of uniqueness. Implicit in many such declarations is the assumption that if we are not the only true Christians, we have no right to exist. Such statements miss the real point.

The fact is that the Churches of Christ *do* exist! We have a rich heritage that belongs to no other group. Our location, our circumstances, our times, our development all make us unique and different from every other religious body. Realizing our identity, with all its strengths and weaknesses, we should be asking whether we are willing to conform to Christ's will for us. Are our hearts turned toward God? Are we striving to be the kind of people God wants us to be? Being unique is not our goal. Being biblical is.

The Restoration Movement, with all its hopes of Christian unity and the conversion of the world, was based on restoring a right relationship between God and humans by means of a proper response to what God has done for us as shown in his Word. The Stone-Campbell Restoration Movement was and is a collective attempt by godly women and men to submit their lives and thought to God's will. As with all humans, their historical and cultural situations influenced their ideas and conclusions. They differed with each other, just as we differ on many things. They were united, however, in their desire to restore a right relationship with the God of Scripture. This would inevitably produce the church as God intended it to be.

Even when we accept God's will, our responses, actions, understandings will never be complete or perfect until we are made perfect in Christ after this life (1 Corinthians 13:12). As we grow in reliance on God's unbounded grace, as we continue to "walk in the light," Jesus' blood must continually do its restoring work. As individual Christians and together as part of Christ's church, we must be engaged in a never-ending quest to grow up into Christ (Ephesians 4:14-15). Pursuit of this goal is the only "right to exist" needed by Churches of Christ. Only if we abandon this aim do we lose the right to exist as Christ's church.

Perhaps we have forgotten that, despite all the pressing problems and gloomy prospects, Christ's church will never cease to exist. It *will* survive (Daniel 2:44). It will do so, not because of our efforts—which often do more harm than good—nor because we are in charge and will see that it survives. It will continue because Christ is in charge. Such a realization does not excuse anyone from the spiritual responsibilities enjoined by Scripture. It does, however, cause us to focus, not on our performance and the necessity of getting everything exactly right—an impossibility for humans—but on the unlimited power of God and His absolute ability to carry out His purposes.

Christ's church is all the people who are held together by a common Redeemer. It is not tied to any century, location, or even worldview. The gospel is as powerful and the church as real in the tents of desert nomads or the huts of village farmers as it is in the high-tech auditoriums of modern city-dwellers. The church "fits" in any age and culture—because what makes it the church is its Lord, who continues his saving work in every age and culture. What makes it the church is the ever-timely message of reconcilation to God through Jesus Christ (2 Corinthians 5:19).

"A house divided against itself cannot stand." Churches of Christ have the message of hope for the world. The reason for our existence is to take that message to those without it. If we cannot manifest the love of God within our ranks, if civil war fragments us into numerous factions, if we are characterized by antagonism and hatred toward one another, then we are in danger of completely obscuring what truly makes the church unique. Larry West, in a 1988 article titled "Civil War in the Kingdom," makes the point well.

> We know how love acts! We know how hate behaves. Love is kind. Hate lifts its ugly head through unkindness. Love is courteous. Hate is rude. If we do not communicate the love of Christ toward one another, even toward the one with whom we disagree the most, we have violated the fundamental doctrine of Christ most assuredly. For to love each other *is* the doctrine of Christ.[37]

Endnotes

[1] Since we reject the authority of written creeds stating specific positions, theological understandings among Churches of Christ can range over a wide spectrum, though there has often been a mainstream or consensus position. See examples of diversity in Leonard Allen, *Distant Voices: Discovering a Forgotten Past for a Changing Church* (Abilene: ACU Press, 1993).

[2] David Edwin Harrell, Jr., "Peculiar People: A Rationale for Modern Conservative Disciples," in *Disciples and the Church Universal,* (Nashville: Disciples of Christ Historical Society, 1967), 35.

[3]The non-institutional division in Churches of of Christ took place in the 1950's principally over whether or not it was scriptural for churches to support extra-congregational institutions like orphans' homes and radio or television ministries. See Steve Wolfgang, "History and Background of the Institutional Controversy," *Guardian of Truth* 33 (April 6, 1989):208-11; (April 20, 1989):240-3; (May 4, 1989):272-5; (May 18, 1989):296-7, 309-10.

[4] See for example, Roy E. Cogdill, *The New Testament Church* (Port Arthur, Texas: O. C. Lambert & Sons, Publishers, 1938); Leroy Brownlow, *Why I Am a Member of the Church of Christ* (Fort Worth, Texas: Leroy Brownlow, 1945); G. C. Brewer, "Is the Church of Christ a Denomination? (n.p., n.d.). All have been reprinted, the first two numerous times.

[5] David Pharr, "Reexamining the Fundamentals, XIII," *Carolina Christian* 32 (April 1990):4.

[6] See for example, D. Gene West, "Is the New Testament Church a Denomination?," *Bible Herald* 36 (May 15, 1989):10-11; Eddie Whitten, "I Love the Church of Christ," *Firm Foundation* 103 (January 14, 1986):3-5.

[7] A few at the extreme right have begun to suggest that "faithful churches" might be forced to use another scriptural name for their congregations if "in the public mind the name 'Church of Christ' refers to what amounts to apostate congregations . . ." Mac Deaver, "On the Name 'Church of Christ,'" *Biblical Notes* 23 (March/April 1994):5.

[8] See for example Calvin Warpula, "The Importance and Uniqueness of the Church," *Image* 2 (July 15, 1986):23.

[9] G. C. Brewer, *A Story of Toil and Tears of*

Love and Laughter: Being the Autobiography of G. C. Brewer (Murfreesboro, TN: DeHoff Publications, 1957), 137-8.

[10] Dub McClish, "Observations on the 'Restoration Summit,'" *Spiritual Sword* 16 (April 1985):21.

[11] G. C. Brewer, "The New Testament Church and Sectarianism," in *Harding College Bible Lectures, 1952* (Austin: Firm Foundation Publishing House, 1952), 165, 176.

[12] Monroe Hawley, *Is Christ Divided? A Study of Sectarianism* (West Monroe, LA: Howard Publishing Company, 1992):98-99.

[13] Anthony L. Dunnavant, "United Christians, Converted World: John 17:20-23 and the Interrelation of Themes in the Campbell-Stone Movement," *Discipliana* 46 (Fall 1986):44-46.

[14] McClish, "Observations on the 'Restoration Summit,'" 21.

[15] See for example the series by Ronnie Morrison, beginning with "Have We Effected Complete Restoration?" *Christian Bible Teacher* 29 (July 1985):272-4; and David Pharr, "Reexamining the Fundamentals, XI," *Carolina Christian* 31 (June 1989):7.

[16] Batsell Barrett Baxter, "Finding the Lord's Church," *Gospel Advocate* 119 (May 12, 1977):289; see also D. Gene West, "Is the New Testament Church a Denomination?" *Bible Herald* 36 (May 15, 1987):11.

[17] See Glover Shipp, "Restoration, An Ongoing Process," *Image* 4 (December 1, 1988):5, 10.

[18] Roy H. Lanier, Jr., "Forum: Letters Demonstrate Wide Diversity of Views from Subscribers," *Christian Chronicle* 49 (May 1992):23.

[19] Paul E. Jarrett, "Our Restoration Heritage,"*Carolina Christian* 30 (June 1988):5-6; F. LaGard Smith, *The Cultural Church* (Nashville: 20th Century Christian, 1992), 209-10.

[20] See Philip Slate, "The Culture Concept and Hermeneutics: Quest to Identify the Permanent in Early Christianity," presented at the Eleventh Annual Christian Scholars Conference, July 18, 1991, David Lipscomb University.

[21] Douglas Hale, "Will We Self-Destruct?" *Restoration Review* 32 (November 1, 1990):375.

[22] David Pharr, "Editor Resigns," *Carolina Christian* 35 (April 1993):3.

[23] Alan E. Highers, "An Evaluation of Our Present Status," *Spiritual Sword* 23 (October 1991):45.

[24] Allan Cloyd, "Unique Contributions in the 19th and 20th Centuries to the Restoration Movement by Non-Instrument Brethren," *Image* 2 (February 15, 1986):27.

[25] Leroy Brownlow, "Why I Am a Member of the Church of Christ," *Magnolia Messenger* 12 (May 1990):6.

[26] Ira Y. Rice, Jr., fund-raising letter, dated February 9, 1992.

[27] F. Furman Kearley, "Signs of Apostasy," *Gospel Advocate* 134 (February 1992):5; Jimmy Jividen, "Using False Teachers," *Gospel Advocate* 134 (February 1992):17-19.

[28] See for example Marc Smith, "Good News From Waco, Texas: Brethren Leaving Institutional Liberalism," *Guardian of Truth* 38 (May 5, 1994):269-271; Fanning Yater Tant, "'Come Back Home'— To What?" *Vanguard* 5 (June 1979):194-6.

[29] Andrew M. Connally, "Radical Liberalism in the Church Today," *Firm Foundation* 103 (March 25, 1986):190.

[30] Jerry Moffitt, "A Call to Arms," *Firm Foundation* 101 (June 26, 1984):303.

[31] Reuel Lemmons, "A Call for Reassessment," *Firm Foundation* 94 (January 25, 1977):50.

[32] Reuel Lemmons, "The Evolution of the Power Structure," *Image* 2 (April 15, 1986):9.

[33] C. Leonard Allen, Richard T. Hughes, Michael R. Weed, *The Worldly Church: A Call for Biblical Renewal* (Abilene: ACU Press, 1988).

[34] Bill Love, *The Core Gospel* (Abilene: ACU Press, 1991).

[35] See Reuel Lemmons, "How to Create a Sect," *Image* 3 (April 15, 1987):4.

[36] Gayle Oler, "What Makes the Church of Christ Different?" *Spritual Sword* 11 (October 1979):42.

[37] Larry West, "Civil War in the Kingdom," *Image* 4 (February 1, 1988):12.

Will the Cycle be Unbroken?

Chapter 4

Schools, Lectureships and Papers: Institutions of Control and Uniformity

Churches of Christ have never had official conventions, assemblies, or conferences. From the earliest days of the Restoration Movement, leaders strongly opposed such denominational organizations as opposed to Scripture and the unity and freedom of Christians. Yet from the beginning we had our own less formal structures that served to hold us together and give us an identity. Sometimes those informal structures have wielded as much power as any official denominational organization.

The major centers of influence and power in Churches of Christ have traditionally been our schools, our national lectureships, and our journals. Of course, in every case it is the administrators and professors, the directors and speakers, and the editors and writers who command the authority. In the past, these leaders would also have been respected gospel preachers and evangelists. Many exercised tremendous influence as they held gospel meetings in all parts of the country.[1] Control in Churches of Christ has been exercised informally, therefore, primarily through schools, lectureships, and journals.

In the past, these institutions usually worked together to create and maintain a consensus on everything from the order and time of worship to positions on theological matters like the premillennial and noninstitutional controversies. Together, they exerted a powerful influence on this group of autonomous congregations, making us amazingly uniform. Those who did not agree with the positions they defined were often excluded from fellowship through the workings of the same institutions.

These institutions remain our informal structures. Today, however, rather than providing cohesion and uniformity, our schools, lectureships and papers have become a gauge of our diversity and fragmentation. None exercises the kind of communion-wide authority once common. New papers, schools and lectureships have risen to challenge older ones. There is a constant barrage of contradictory messages from the increasingly different institutions. What can we learn about our present situation from these important entities?

Higher Education: Source of Problems or the Solution?

There is no doubt in the minds of some that the Christian colleges have been a major source of what they view as apostasy. In a 1986 article titled "From Whence Cometh False Teaching Among Us?" the author charged that the breeding grounds of apostasy and digression are some of our schools and papers. He singled out specific schools as the sources of false teaching on marriage, divorce and remarriage, the Holy Spirit, evolution, and grace. One school, he asserted, "has been known for some time as a hot bed of liberalism," and since its former dean was going to serve as president of still another university, he stated that anyone who ever expected anything good from it could dash those expectations. He concluded by urging his readers to withhold support from institutions they feel are no longer answerable to faithful members of the Lord's Church.[2]

Another writer charged that the schools had gone the way of digression, liberalism, apostasy, false doctrines, compromise, smugness and conceit.

> The administrations of these schools simply refuse to give you a decent response to that about which you ask. The classic response from a college official goes something like this. "Thank you for your letter. We are doing a great work. We would like to have you visit our campus. Pray for us." That is about as close to [an answer to] an inquiry on doctrinal matters being taught at the school as one can expect.[3]

The entire July, 1991 issue of *The Spiritual Sword,* published in Memphis, Tennessee, centered on "Christian Schools—Opportunities, Benefits and Dangers." The editor was careful to emphasize that he endorsed Christian education, yet there were some disturbing trends he felt needed attention. Articles in the issue focused on the teaching of modernism and evolution in the schools, particularly as those ideas eroded confidence in the authority and infallibility of Scripture. He concluded by urging readers to send their children to faithful Christian schools for an education, but to withhold financial support and their children "when and if a school ceases to stand for the principles which we all hold dear."[4]

In a booklet published the following summer, titled "The Worldly University: The Apostasy of ACU," the authors concluded that they could endorse none of the Christian colleges and universities in existence. They recommended that parents send their children

> to a faithful two-year school of Bible studies. . . and then go ahead and send your kids to a state school. . . . . the false teaching in a state school is not as subtle as in a "Christian university." It is a lot easier to see a rock coming toward your face than it is to see a snake in the grass waiting to bite your heel. . . . there are no other Christian institutions of higher learning that we would recommend.[5]

A frequent accusation made against the schools is that they have been unfaithful to the aims and goals of their original founders.[6] School officials have uniformly responded that while many externals have changed through the years, their faithfulness to the Christian ideals of the founders has not.[7]

Harold Hazelip, President of David Lipscomb University in Nashville, presented a series of four position papers connected with the school's Centennial Celebration in early 1991. One was subtitled "Methods may change with time, but the purpose of David Lipscomb University remains unchanged." He stated Lipscomb's mission as "to help students become Christlike through a daily study of the Bible and other courses necessary for growing in usefulness, good citizenship, and in Christian influence on society." Hazelip said that to carry out this purpose, the school must change its approaches to educating students so that their education will be relevant to the time in which they live. Quoting Oliver Wendell Holmes, Hazelip agreed that "To reach the port of heaven, we must sail sometimes with the wind and sometimes against it—but we must sail, and not drift, nor lie at anchor."[8]

At the 1993 Abilene Christian University Lectures, President Royce Money delivered a major address titled "On This Rock." In the speech Money admitted that the university had not been as responsive to the churches as it should have. He went on to assert, however, that every faculty member was deeply committed to Jesus Christ, the church and to the inspiration and authority of every word of Scripture. He concluded, ". . . you will be better served to get your information about ACU from ACU and not from some critical brotherhood paper. You will have to make up your mind which one to believe. You cannot believe both."[9]

Part of the Restoration Movement, as well as American religion generally, has a history of nervousness about and even hostility toward higher education. Our forebears often reflected this suspicion in their hostility toward college-trained preachers and the dangers of studying in theological seminaries—or as they were often called, theological cemeteries.[10] Jaroslav Pelikan, historian of Christian doctrine at Yale University, has observed that most religious bodies "remain fundamentally ambiguous about scholarship. Many are eager to use it when it supports their settled positions, but they become skittish when it moves into uncharted areas."[11]

Sociological data indicates that the more educated populations in American religion are the least conservative. In a study of why people leave religious groups, for example, Wade Clark Roof and Kirk Hadaway conclude that

> Higher education tends to expand one's horizons and may also mean greater exposure to countercultural values. For many persons, such exposure has worked to erode traditional plausibility structures, which maintained poorly understood religious convictions.[12]

The status of our Christian colleges and universities is and will continue to be a significant factor in the division or avoidance of division in our ranks. Robert Wuthnow suggests that in American religion as a whole,

> If any segment of the evangelical community has the opportunity to gain understanding of the present religious conflicts and to contribute to their resolution, it should be . . .the social science faculties of the nation's evangelical colleges.[13]

Certainly we must not be fooled into thinking that scholars are superior human beings. Intellectuals are no better than anyone else. To quote Peter Berger, intellectuals "are capable of the most mindless fanaticisms."[14] On the other hand, we must not idealize ignorance and lack of education. The dedicated Christians who are also scholars teaching in our schools and our pulpits and writing in our papers can help us understand and resolve our conflicts. No, we cannot solve our problems with detached intellectual activity. We must, however, encourage and support our godly, spiritual, committed scholars to grapple head-on with the difficult questions being posed in real-life situations. The questions are not simple, they will not go away, and they cannot be ignored. Our

Christian schools and Christian scholars can and must be part of the solution.

Lectureships: Our National "Conventions"

Another gauge of our shape and direction is our lectureships. A careful look at the speakers, topics, and numbers in attendance over the past two decades makes a gripping study in diversity.

Traditionally, the largest and most influential lectureships have been organized and conducted by our colleges and universities. Many of these gatherings have been in existence for well over half a century. Abilene Christian University conducted its 76th annual Bible Lectureship in 1994, Harding University its 71st, David Lipscomb its 66th, Freed-Hardeman its 58th, and Pepperdine its 51st. These gatherings have attracted thousands of Christians yearly and feature the most prominent and respected leaders in Churches of Christ.

While our lectureships have no official status or legislative powers, they certainly provide a forum for noted preachers to assert their conclusions on a range of theological topics, from the routine to the controversial. With audiences from all parts of the country, the powerfully presented positions are often carried back to local congregations and preached to many thousands more.

William S. Banowsky contended in his 1965 book *Mirror of a Movement,* that the Abilene Christian Lectureship, then the largest of our gatherings, was the "chief vehicle for the communication of ideas" in Churches of Christ.

> The Lectureship, without becoming a policy-making conference, has filled a crucial vacuum by providing a medium for brotherhood-wide fellowship and stimulation. . . . the Lectureship has been the most vital pulpit of a pulpit-sparked movement. It has been the vanguard of the church's phenomenal growth.[15]

Banowsky's main point was that by examining the contents of the sermons presented over the years, one could get a feel for the nature and direction of the movement. The theological emphases, the changes, the controversies—all are reflected in the Lectureship. The same might also have been claimed for other college lectureships like those at Harding and Freed-Hardeman Universities.[16]

Today, no single lectureship is an accurate reflection of the entire communion. The college and university lectureships continue to draw crowds, the largest being Pepperdine and Abilene Christian, with thousands from across the country and the world. Among the gatherings with the highest attendance, however, have been the Tulsa Soul-Winning Workshop (begun in 1976) and the Nashville Jubilee (begun in 1989), consistently drawing from eight to ten thousand persons or more. Both programs have highlighted positive ways in which Christians can share their faith and grow spiritually.

These and the university lectureships have been boycotted in recent years by some who see them as heretical. Some of the dissenters have begun their own alternative meetings, often sponsored by schools of preaching or local congregations. Among these lectureships are those of the Florida School of Preaching (Lakeland, Florida), Memphis School of Preaching, the Annual Robertson County (Tennessee) Lectureship, and the Annual Denton (Texas) Lectures.[17]

Even a cursory examination of the programs of these and similar lectureship for the last decade reveals the concerns they are designed to meet. Themes have included such titles as "Is Today's Church Contending for the Faith?" "Current Issues Facing the Church," "Renewed Emphasis on Fundamentals of the Faith," "The Militant Church," "The Church Challenged by Current Issues," "Liberalism," "Back to the Basics," "The Things Most Surely Believed," "Issues Facing the Church," "Grace Only?" "Issues and Answers," "The Current Digression," Critical Issues Facing the Church," "Issues that Still Confront Us," "The Current Digression Continues," "The Old Paths," "Contending for the Faith," "Forward with the Fundamentals," and "Challenges to the Faith."[18]

Even when the lectureship themes seem more constructive in tone, an examination of the program reveals the same thrust. One gathering with the theme "The Church Enters the Twenty-First Century" included speeches on "Preparing for a Smaller Brotherhood," "The Remnant Must be Militant," "The Emergence of a New Denomination from Within the Lord's Church," "The New Hermeneutic: a Doctrine to Make the Divine Pattern of None Effect," "False Doctrine in Our Bible Class Literature," "May One Church Withdraw Fellowship from a Sister Congregation?" and "Come Ye Out from Among Them and Be Ye Separate."[19]

Programs from gatherings like the Tulsa, Middle Tennessee and International Bible College Workshops, Jubilee, and the David Lipscomb and Oklahoma Christian University Lectures include topics like "Master, Here Am I," "Jesus, the Light of the World," "Our God is Alive," "His Truth Is Marching On," "Moving Into the Heart of Jesus," "So Loved He the World," "The Restoration of the Christian Home," "Room in the Kingdom," "Unto Love and Good Works," "Mobilizing for Evangelism," "Be of Good Courage," "Building on Our Strengths," "The Practice of Pure Religion," "Lights in a World of Darkness," "Room at the Cross," and "What's Right With the Church."

The contrast between the two groups is striking. The first is clearly preoccupied with what it sees as dangerous departures from faith by a significant part of Churches of Christ. It is compelled to try to stop this apostasy by exposing it at every opportunity. The other group, judging from the lecture themes, sees no departure from faith. Rather, it sees the danger in each individual failing to grow spiritually and evangelize the lost. These themes are not mutually exclusive, but it is a matter of emphasis. Each group likely could learn much from the other. But only if they would carefully and lovingly listen to each other, presenting their views in a way that did not judge the other's motives and character.

In reality, the picture emerging from our lectureships is not one of two easily identifiable groups. There are literally hundreds of gatherings every year, many of which are not clearly associated with either of the tendencies above. At least six types of lectureships and workshops exist: (1) those connected to our colleges and universities, (2) those conducted by Bible colleges and schools of preaching, (3) evangelism/soul-winning workshops and seminars and missions forums, (4) specialized meetings such as those on church growth, worship, music, single parents, and current issues, (5) city/ regional/ international gatherings, (6) family-oriented conferences and encampments.

One thing is clear, however: no single lectureship or category of lectureships can be said to be representative of all Churches of Christ. The differences in emphasis, the mutual disapproval, the increase in the number of gatherings—all indicate a pulling apart and separation of sisters and brothers. We must now ask, what are the specific issues over which we have come to such disagreement?

Issues and Papers: Right to Left

The surest way to determine details of what issues are important to us is to examine our periodicals. Since our papers, like all our institutions, are private operations, they usually take on the character of their editors. These editors often exercise great influence on their readers and sometimes have been referred to as "editor-bishops" in larger Restoration history.[20] Like the lectureships, however, there has been in recent years a tremendous increase in the number of publications and a dilution of influence.

A survey of several of our major publications for the past decade yielded the following list of issues that were discussed by at least some in Churches of Christ. The list is not meant to cover every possible controversy, nor is it ordered in any special way. It does record issues that were important enough to be matters of fellowship for some.

1. The use of "modern" translations of the Bible. Some object to versions like the New International and Today's English, often defending the exlusive use of the King James and American Standard.

2. The construction of gymnasiums and recreational facilities by churches. A range of practices was labelled "gimmick Christianity" by opponents, including church sports teams and holding of community functions in the building.

3. The precise understanding of the the biblical account of creation. Some opposed any position that would allow the possibility of micro-evolution (small changes within species) and those like John Clayton who would support it.

4. The use of separate worship assemblies for young children, as well as any "cell-based" or small group meetings that take the place of the corporate worship assembly.

5. The presence or absence of false teachers among the faculty of our colleges, focusing especially on the Bible and biology departments. Specific cases at David Lipscomb and Abilene Christian Universities were particularly heated.

6. The Crossroads/Boston philosophy of evangelism and church organization, and the seeming endorsement of the movement by prominent mainstream congregations and preachers, particularly the White's Ferry Road and Garnett Road churches, Alvin Jennings and the *Christian Chronicle*.

7. The non-distinctive nature of the Herald of Truth, focusing especially on the "Heartbeat" program with Landon Saunders that did not explicitly mention Churches of Christ.

8. The marriage, divorce and remarriage controversy, particularly dealing with the views of James D. Bales that those outside the church (aliens) are not under the Christian laws of marriage.[21]

9. Restoration Forum meetings with members of the independent Christian Churches, sometimes called the "New Unity Movement," were praised as a move toward the unity Christ commanded between brothers and sisters and attacked as an unfaithful compromising with apostates. Attacks were directed at, among others, Rubel Shelly, Alan Cloyd, and Marvin Phillips.

10. The nature of the authority of elders was a significant issue. Some rejected the model of a corporate board, denying elders had any authority over a congregation but were instead to lead by being examples of loving sacrifice and service. Others insisted elders had absolute authority from God to make decisions in all matters not specified by scripture.

11. The matter of where to draw clear scriptural lines of fellowship was raised, sparked partially by the Restoration Forum talks with the conservative Christian Churches. Rubel Shelly articulated a position that recognized different levels of fellowship which some attacked as unscriptural.

12. An old controversy concerning how much one must know at the time of baptism regained attention. Specifically, the question was whether the person must know that baptism is for the remission of sins at the time of the immersion for it to be valid. Might baptism for any scriptural reason (including simply because God commanded it) be sufficient?

13. The nature of worship became a topic of heated debate. Among the issues was the precise definition of worship (in and outside the assembly), the use of choirs and soloists in worship assemblies, the use of drama, and other non-traditional activities.

14. Questions were raised about the traditional

methods of biblical interpretation among Churches of Christ. A "New Hermeneutic" (actually several alternative approaches) was suggested to replace or supplement the perceived older method of discerning direct commands, apostolic examples and necessary inferences. Some saw the questioning as a rejection of the inerrancy of Scripture and the New Testament as our pattern. The use of biblical critical methods for interpretation was also a matter of concern for some.

15. The role of women in the public function of the churches became an increasingly volatile issue, with several publications and widely publicized lectures reexamining traditional positions and interpretations.[22]

16. Our large national gatherings, particularly the Tulsa Soul-Winning Workshop and the Nashville Jubilee, enjoyed large crowds and provoked attacks from some who labelled them forums for false teachers and practices.

17. The use of instrumental music in worship, though almost universally rejected by Churches of Christ, was increasingly regarded as a non-salvation issue, prompting some to reexamine our traditional position and others to champion it strongly.[23]

18. There was controversy in some circles concerning the appropriateness of clapping and raising hands in worship services.

19. The role of the Holy Spirit in conversion and in the life of the Christian continued to be debated. The question especially centered on whether the Spirit can and does operate apart from the written Word.

20. The increasing frequency of participation by some congregations with other religious groups in

activities and joint worship services heightened tensions in areas where such activities took place.[24]

Many other controversies fit either into the category of personal matters, usually connected with one or more of the above concerns,[25] or moral issues, such as the need for strong homes, where basic agreement exists. The more difficult ethical issues like homosexuality and abortion received relatively little attention.[26]

There are clear progressive and traditional positions on each of these twenty issues, though some are more difficult to categorize (i.e., the Crossroads/Boston movement). We can begin to get a picture of the shape of Churches of Christ today by determining how many hold progressive positions on these issues and how many hold the traditional stances. Though it is not a scientifically accurate method, one of of the few ways we have of getting some feel for how many support specific positions is by defining the positions of our journals, then gauging the support for each by measuring its readership.

Of course, people subscribe to papers they don't always agree with, and some read a variety of journals that take opposite positions on many issues. These facts must make us cautious about reading too much into the following data. Nevertheless, this survey of some of our major representative journals can begin to give us a feel for our current shape. [For a graphic representation of this analysis, please refer to the chart on the next page.]

What can be said about Churches of Christ from this information? Interpreting the data is more difficult than putting it together. Some trends are reflected, but other significant ones are not. Chapters

ISSUES AND PERIODICALS: A HINT AT THE SHAPE OF CHURCHES OF CHRIST

CC—Christian Chronicle (editor, Howard Norton)
CFTF—Contending for the Faith (editor, Ira Y. Rice, Jr.)
FF—Firm Foundation (editor, Buster Dobbs)
GA—Gospel Advocate (editor, Furman Kearley)
IM—Image (editor, Denny Boultinghouse)
21CC—21st Century Christian (editor, Prentice Meador, Jr.)
WE—World Evangelist (editor, Basil Overton)
WS—Wineskins (editors, Mike Cope, Rubel Shelly, Phillip
Morrison)

Issues

1. Use of modern translations
2. Gymnasiums and "gimmicks"
3. Possibility of micro-evolution
4. Cell-based or small group worship
5. Fidelity of Christian college faculty
6. Crossroads/Boston movement
7. Herald of Truth's aproach to evangelism
8. The "Bales" view of marriage, divorce
   and remarriage
9. Restoration Forums with conservative
   Christian Churches

10. Change in concept of authority of elders
11. The existence of levels of fellowship
12. Any scriptural reason sufficient for
    valid baptism
13. Innovations in style and concept of
    worship (worship as all of life)
14. Reexamination of traditional hermeneutic
15. Expanded public role of women
16. Large non-traditional lectureships
17. Instrumental music in worship
18. Handclapping in worship
19. Role of the Holy Spirit beyond the
    written word
20. Participation in religious activities
    with other religious groups

Responses

1=Strongly For

2=For

3=Not an Issue

4=Against

5=Strongly Against

Editorial content of publications (from 1980 to the present) was analyzed to determine responses to 20 issues listed at left. Numerical scores were tallied according to line graph below. Lower scores would tend to indicate a more "progressive" or "liberal" stance. Higher scores would indicate a more "traditional" or "conservative" position.

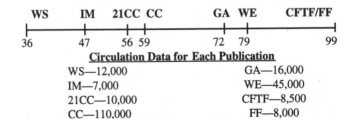

WS	IM	21CC	CC	GA	WE	CFTF/FF
36	47	56	59	72	79	99

Circulation Data for Each Publication

WS—12,000	GA—16,000
IM—7,000	WE—45,000
21CC—10,000	CFTF—8,500
CC—110,000	FF—8,000

Five and Six deal with some of those other important factors. In the meantime, there are several observations that can be made from this information.

1. Based on a membership of 1.25 million for Churches of Christ, the journal of largest circulation among us (*Christian Chronicle*) has a subscription list of less than 9% of the membership. *World Evangelist* has a little more than 3%, while *Gospel Advocate* has slightly above a 1% share. The others average well under 1%. Assuming that each issue is read by between 2 and 3 people (the industry standard), that still leaves a vast majority that have no direct contact with any of these major papers. Any conclusions about the strength of certain positions based on this information must be made with great caution. However, in the absence of a scientifically conducted nationwide survey of our members, this is the most accurate picture available of this subject matter.

2. Many other papers are not listed above. The most recent edition of the *Yearbook of American and Canadian Churches* lists sixteen major papers. The Christian College Librarians regularly index almost 100 non-local papers published by members of Churches of Christ. Some, like *World Radio News* and the *International Gospel Hour News,* are published by specific ministries. Others have special audiences, such as *Christian Woman* and *Christian Echo* (published by black churches). Still others, like *Leaven* and *Christian Bible Teacher,* are aimed at ministers and teachers. Often, the unique thrust of these papers means they do not deal with the issues we identified and would be more difficult to place on the spectrum.

Others, however, like *Spiritual Sword* and

Biblical Notes, are oriented toward doctrinal issues and clearly fit on the conservative end of the continuum. Papers that reflect more progressive attitudes include *Integrity,* published in Michigan and *Ensign,* published in Alabama. The list changes every year, with some papers dying and others beginning.

3. With all the cautions given, it seems from the chart that most members of Churches of Christ fit into a broad, moderate position. *Every* position taken on the issues listed above would be classified as conservative in the wider religious world, yet there is a significant difference between the two ends of our spectrum. We have always been diverse. Now, however, we are being pulled increasingly toward the extremes, where, too often, hatred, misunderstanding and bigotry are allowed to breed.

Since most members of Churches of Christ do not read any of the major journals, the vast majority will go the direction of the leadership of their congregation, whether that be the eldership or a strongly persuasive preacher. Leaders must guard against divisive forces that obscure the gospel and pull them toward extremes. There are too may positive dirctions available to us to permit us to allow the cycle of division to continue.

The Role of Our Institutions

Our institutions will be either points around which various factions rally or voices calling for spiritual reconciliation. As has been seen, it is already possible to identify real differences on the issues. Difference, however, does not have to mean division. If, in addition to an attitude of submission to God and to his will as expressed in the authoritative Word we add an unswerving commitment to love one another and build one another up, the cycle can be broken.

Endnotes

[1] The role of the traveling evangelist has been greatly diminished because of the demise of the Gospel Meeting. In the past, men like Horace Busby, Roy Cogdill, Sr., Foy E. Wallace, Jr., Guy N. Woods and others helped maintain doctrinal uniformity in the churches through their wide contact with congregations and the great respect they commanded.

[2] Ernest S. Underwood, "From Whence Cometh False Teaching Among Us?" *Contending for the Faith* 17(June 1986):8.

[3] James W. Boyd, "Major Source of Digression," *Contending for the Faith* 19(August 1988):8.

[4] Alan E. Highers, "Christian Schools—Positives and Negatives," *Spiritual Sword* 22 (July 1991):3.

[5] Kevin Cauley and Cleo Reeder, *The Worldly University: The Apostasy of A.C.U.* (Austin, TX: Biblical Notes, 1992), 78.

[6] See for example Roy Deaver, "Forward," in "The Worldly University," pp. 5-7; and William Woodson, "The Aims of the Founders," *Spiritual Sword* 22 (July 1991):7-10.

[7] Many of the Christian colleges could cite instances, some very recent, of the firing of faculty and administrators for holding positions that differed from those of the controlling parties.

[8] Harold Hazelip, "3,825 Souls, One Mission," A Position Paper for the Centennial Celebration of David Lipscomb University, 1991.

[9] Royce Money, "On This Rock I Will Build

My Church," Presented at the ACU Bible Lecture-ship, February 21, 1993. See also the replies to Money's speech by Roy Deaver, Thomas B. Warren, and Mac Deaver, "On This Rock I Will Build My Church," *Contending for the Faith* 24 (May 1993):1-19.

[10] Richard Mouw, "Why Do Evangelicals Need the Academy?" *Christianity Today* 34 (October 8, 1990):86.

[11] Mark Noll, "The Doctrine Doctor," *Christianity Today* 34 (September 10, 1990):25.

[12] C. Kirk Hadaway and Wade Clark Roof, "Apostasy in American Churches: Evidence from National Survey Data," in *Falling From the Faith: Causes and Consequences of Religious Apostasy*, ed. David G. Bromley (Newbury Park, CA: Sage Publications, Inc., 1988), 36.

[13] Robert Wuthnow, *The Struggle for America's Soul: Evangelicals, Liberals, and Secularism* (Grand Rapids: William B. Eerdmans Publishing Company, 1989), 159.

[14] Peter L. Berger, "Worldly Wisdom, Christian Foolishness," *First Things* (August/September 1990):21.

[15] William S. Banowsky, *The Mirror of a Movement: Churches of Christ as Seen Through the Abilene Christian College Lectureship* (Dallas: Christian Publishing Company, 1965), x.

[16] Morris Lynn McCauley, "Freed-Hardeman College Lectures, 1969-1970: Rhetoric of Reaction" (M.A. thesis, Louisiana State University, 1972); Richard H. Chastain, "An Analysis of the Issues and Ideas Presented Through the Abilene Christian University Lectures (1965-1982)"(M.A. thesis, Abilene

Christian University, 1983).

[17] See Ira Y. Rice, Jr., "Battle of the Lectureships, Jubilees and Workshops," *Contending for the Faith* 21 (May 1990):2.

[18] Themes selected from a survey of lectureship announcements in various journals between 1980 and 1990.

[19] Advertisement for Houston College of the Bible Lectures, *Contending for the Faith* 25 (April 1994):15.

[20] See William T. Moore, *Comprehensive History of the Disciples of Christ* (New York: Fleming H. Revell, 1909), 699. In 1986 the Forrest F. Reed Lectures of the Disciples of Christ Historical Society focused on the role of three important "editor-bishops," including David Lipscomb. See Richard T. Hughes, Henry E. Webb, Howard E. Short, *The Power of the Press* (Nashville: Disciples of Christ Historical Society, 1987).

[21] See James D. Bales, *Not Under Bondage* (Searcy, AR: J. D. Bales, 1979).

[22] See especially Carroll D. Osburn, ed., *Essays On Women in Earliest Christianity* (Joplin, MO: College Press, 1993); *Gender and Ministry: The Role of the Woman in the Work and Worship of the Church*, Freed-Hardeman Preachers' and Church Workers' Forum, 1990 (Huntsville, AL: Publishing Designs, Inc., 1990).

[23] A front-page article in the *Jackson* (Tennesee) *Sun* for February 7, 1994, "An Instrumental Debate: Church of Christ to Discuss Permitting Instrumentation in Worship Services," told of a forum on instrumental music at the Freed-Hardeman Lectureship and quoted a University spokesperson that

5% to 6% of our congregations use instruments in worship. See J. E. Choate and William Woodson, *Sounding Brass and Clanging Symbols: The History and Significance of Instrumental Music in the Restoration Movement, 1827-1968* (Henderson, TN: Freed-Hardeman University, 1990).

[24] See for example Lucille Prince, "Historic Event: Church of Christ, Methodist Church Hold Joint Meeting," *Times-Daily* (Florence, Alabama) (September 25, 1993):4B-5B; F. Furman Kearley, "Unity Desired But Not Essential," *Magnolia Messenger* 15 (July/August 1993):1.

[25]Some of the most heated of these were the controversy surrounding Rubel Shelley (especially beginning with his book *I Just Want to be a Christian*), the beginning of two new journals (*Image* in 1985 and *Wineskins* in 1992) that consciously provided a forum for more progressive voices, and the replacement of Guy N. Woods as editor of the *Gospel Advocate,* leading some to question the reliability of the "old reliable."

[26] See Craig Churchill, "Churches of Christ and Abortion: A Survey of Selected Periodicals," unpublished paper, Abilene Christian University, May 1994.

Chapter 5

The Complicated Patterns
of Current Division

In 1939 James DeForest Murch attempted to chart the spectrum of the Restoration Movement in his day in an article in the *Christian Standard*.[1] He chose, as we did in the previous chapter, to focus on the positions of the prominent papers on twenty-three doctrinal and theological matters. These items ranged from the deity of Christ and inspiration of the Scriptures to the use of preachers' lists and individual communion cups. His characterization was, like ours so far, on a scale from right to left. Even Murch recognized, however, that things were more complicated than that. Each of the doctrines or beliefs had several shades of understanding he was not able to portray on his chart.

Things have become even more complicated since Murch's attempt to portray the shape of the movement. A second major split in the Restoration Movement was made formal in 1968 with the formation of the Christian Church (Disciples of Christ). Congregations that rejected its denominational structure requested to be dropped from the listing in the Disciples Yearbook, forming a fellowship of conservative Christian Churches.[2]

Churches of Christ have grown rapidly and become increasingly diverse in the half-century since Murch's article—reflecting the increasingly diverse American religious scene generally. The following attempt to map the shape of contemporary Churches of Christ is not totally satisfactory. Like Murch's earlier effort, it cannot take into account every relevant factor. It is something like looking at a wafer-thin slice of the globe. Yet, based on years of intimate familiarity with Churches of Christ, the chart on the facing page does reflect some of the major identifiable tendencies today. At least it may help us understand our current shape as we consider and react to it.

Explanation of Terms

The left-to-right axis on the chart contains elements that would be expected in any such description. Please remember, however, that the chart as a whole reflects all of American religion. The shaded circle that defines Churches of Christ is almost entirely on the conservative side of the vertical line. The following definitions represent the poles, the extremes of each axis. They are, therefore, stereotypes that fit no one perfectly. Rather, they represent tendencies that characterize certain positions to a greater or lesser degree.

Liberalism has a very high view of human ability, yet also has a wide view of the grace of God that allows for imperfections and failure. Liberals are

Chart: Visible Groupings in Churches of Christ

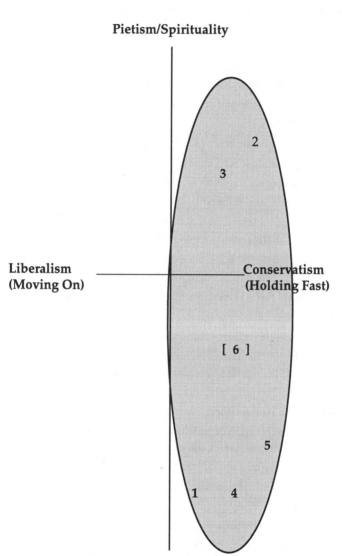

Pietism/Spirituality

2

3

Liberalism
(Moving On)

Conservatism
(Holding Fast)

[6]

5

1   4

Intellectualism

characterized by a low emphasis on doctrinal precision and uniformity, viewing the formulation of doctrine as a human activity. They understand the authority of Scripture in a moral rather than a legal sense; that is, Scripture functions by motivating people to want to live moral lives rather than by imposing a strict legal code. Too often, liberals ignore the feelings or relevance of their more conservative brothers and sisters.

Conservatism places much importance on doctrinal precision and correctness and views the Bible as a legal document to which all must strictly adhere. This tendency generally takes a low view of human nature. Yet, those at the extreme have very high expectations that everyone can and must understand and act on the truth in a near perfect way (usually, according to a preferred conservative interpretation). Any who fail to live up to those expectations will feel the wrath of the leaders. Too often, conservatives make negative judgments on the motives and character of their brothers and sisters to the left.

The vertical line could be labelled the "heart and head" axis. *Pietism* is a label well known to anyone who has studied church history. Originally attached to the movement that reacted to the cold, ritualistic religion developing after the Protestant Reformation, it refers generally to an emphasis on the Spirit of God in the life of the Christian. It is not an inwardly directed, "mystical" experience. Rather, pietism stresses the importance of doing good for others— living a visibly godly life as empowered and directed by the Holy Spirit. Scripture is very important to pietists, but is often interpreted spiritually rather than legalistically. There is much emphasis on feeling and doing, and on the need for the constant, direct and personal guidance of God's Spirit.

Intellectualism's most obvious trait is the importance it places on human understanding and mental ability. Scripture is handled in a careful, scholarly way, understood as an intellectual document to be examined in minute detail for its meaning. Intellectuals tend to have a high view of human ability to reason and understand.

Using these four tendencies as a matrix, it is possible to identify at least six groupings within Churches of Christ today, identified by the numbers on the chart. The inside of the shaded circle represents the membership of Churches of Christ. There is no way, other than the attempt in the last chapter, to measure the relative strength of any position. There are probably congregations that would, as a unit, fit each description, but it is more likely that individual members with leanings toward the different positions can be found in most congregations. The positions labelled on the chart do not neatly encompass every member or congregation of Churches of Christ. There is much space between each number. Nevertheless, these are discernible forces pulling in several different directions.

1. The "progressives" tend to be highly educated, well-read, and possess a high degree of social consciousness. Most would have supported *Mission* magazine before its demise. Journals such as *Integrity* and *Leaven* receive their support now. Many who participate in the yearly Christian Scholars Conferences would be included in this category, though that group is extremely diverse and includes persons from other groupings as well. Remember that this grouping is still quite moderate when placed on the larger spectrum of American religion.

2. Those in the "pietistic" group tend to emphasize spirituality and godly living over precise doctrinal formulations, yet are quite conservative on fundamental doctrines and literalistic in their interpretation of Scripture. They tend to be more open to cooperation with like-minded members of other churches, especially in benevolent works and in small group Bible studies and prayer meetings. They are not the charismatics of the 1960's and 1970's, though some might be characterized as part of the "third wave" of the Holy Spirit.[3] Some tend to be intolerant of those who do not put the same emphasis on the kinds of spirituality they see as important. Activities such as the "Room at the Inn" program in various cities fit in this category, though again, not all who participate in this program are "pietists." A concerted effort to introduce ministers in Churches of Christ to charismatic and "third wave" theology through an annual Conference of Spiritual Renewal has been conducted in recent years by Jim Bevis and others connected with the Belmont Church in Nashville, Tennessee.

3. "Evangelicals" see themselves as part of the larger conservative-to-moderate constellation in American religion. Leaders attend interdenominational functions, such as ministers' lectureships and church growth seminars. They are often more aware of trends and resources in the larger evangelical world than they are of matters in Churches of Christ. Evangelical megachurches like Willow Creek in suburban Chicago tend to be their model, though not all their congregations are large. Several younger, very talented ministers of large churches, as well as many members of these churches, fit this category. While some seem at the fringes of Churches of Christ, most will remain and have much influence in our current troubles. Ministers like Max Lucado and Mike Cope might be placed here.

4. "Neo-Conservatives" have emerged in recent years from the progressive and intellectual tendencies. They are fearful of moves being made by our "progressives" and "pietists" (perhaps without distinguishing the groups), which they believe are moves away from correct positions in worship, doctrine and organization. They must be classed as reactionaries, yet they do not take the harsher position of the "fundamentalists." Many were trained in liberal seminaries, tended to accept liberal theology, but saw some of its fruits and have reacted against it. One self-professed neo-conservative sees some in the forefront of innovation in Churches of Christ to be part of "dysfunctional" churches—hardly ones to be giving the rest of us advice about how to shape the future of the movement. They often take traditional doctrinal positions, but have come to these conclusions through non-traditional methods. This has made them suspect to the "fundamentalists." James Thompson of Abilene Christian University and Michael Weed of the Institute for Christian Studies in Austin, Texas are representatives of this category.

5. The "fundamentalists" are extreme, conservative traditionalists. They generally insist on conformity to their doctrinal conclusions and actively target those they see as threats to the church. They tend to draw lines of fellowship to exclude all who do not agree with their understandings and formulations. Our fundamentalists include editors Ira Rice of *Contending for the Faith*, Buster Dobbs of *Firm Foundation*, and Roy Deaver of *Biblical Notes*, as well as teachers and preachers like Thomas B. Warren and Garland Elkins. "Fundamentalism" in American religion is a movement that began around the turn of the century and includes a wide variety of religious groups with whom those listed would certainly not identify. The definition used here is the one formulated by the Fundamentalism Project that identifies exclusivity and militancy as main characteristics of all fundamentalists.[4]

6. Finally, there exists a large group of "moderates" whose leaders intentionally counsel against reactionary stances. These leaders try to point out good and bad tendencies in the identifiable groupings and see themselves as serving a peacemaking function. They are very conservative in the larger context. A spectrum exists within this group, with some more conservative than others. Among the leaders are Howard Norton of *Christian Chronicle*, Neil Anderson and Furman Kearley of *Gospel Advocate*, and Cecil May of Magnolia Bible College.[5] This group is especially vulnerable to attacks by all extremes and the temptation to become reactionary is acute.[6]

Once again, all of these positions and the spaces between them define a body of religious "conservatives." The tensions that exist in Churches of Christ do not involve "conservatives" and "liberals"— as those terms are normally used—moving away from each other. Instead, they involve conservatives separating from other conservatives. Some leaders have accused persons with whom they disagree of not believing in the authority of Scripture. The people involved in our present controversies are not liberals in such a theological sense. Such imprecise accusations serve to worsen our difficulties and further the process of alienation. Some will certainly disagree vehemently with the contention that liberalism is not our current menace. Many insist that we are now facing the same kind of theological liberalism that led to division with the Christian Church a century ago. There are definite similarities, but there is also a fundamental difference in circumstances that we must now examine.

Endnotes

[1] James DeForest Murch, "Oursel's As Ithers See Us," *Christian Standard* 74(March 18, 1939): 246-64.

[2] See Ronald E. Osborn, "The Irony of the Twentieth-Century Christian Church (Disciples of Christ): Making it to the Mainline Just at the Time of Disestablishment," *Mid-Stream* 28 (July 1989): 293-312.

[3] "Third wave" refers to a movement among members of mainline and evangelical churches who, while rejecting the excesses of Pentecostal and Charismatic theology and practice, believe in the active work of the Holy Spirit in the lives of Christians today.

[4] Martin E. Marty and R. Scott Appleby, eds., *Fundamentalisms Observed* (Chicago: University of Chicago Press, 1991); see James Stephen Wolfgang, "Fundamentalism and the Churches of Christ, 1910-1930" (M.A. Thesis, Vanderbilt University, 1990).

[5] See for example Cecil May, "Is Division Imminent?" *Preacher Talk* 8 (May 1992):1; Glenn

Jarrett, "GA Editor Pleads for 'Balance' At MBC Forum," *The Magnolia Messenger* 15 (October 1992):1, 14.

[6] A major grouping that does not fit this theological listing is the African-American Churches of Christ. With over 1200 US congregations, African-American churches support a college (Southwestern Christian) in Terrell, Texas, a paper (the *Christian Echo*) published since the early 1900's, an Annual National Lectureship since 1945, an annual youth conference, and a biannual evangelistic crusade. See Robert E. Hooper, *A Distinct People: A History of Churches of Christ in the Twentieth Century* (West Monroe, LA: Howard Publishing Company, 1993), chapter twelve, "Out of Bondage: Black Churches of Christ in America." The January 1990 issue of the *Gospel Advocate,* titled "Divided We Stand: Overcoming Racial Prejudice in the Church," contained four incisive articles by African-American leaders dealing with the history of these congregations and solutions to the practical division that exists between us. These churches are generally very conservative theologically, though culturally having much in common with most African-American religious groups.

Chapter 6

The 1890's and the 1990's:
So Alike, Yet So Different

For several years in journal articles and conversations, many have expressed the concern that Churches of Christ today face the same situation that confronted the Restoration Movement at the end of the 19th century. They fear that theological liberals who do not take seriously the inspiration and authority of Scripture are threatening the very identity of the church. These liberals, the argument goes, are leading undiscerning Christians down the same path taken a century ago by the Disciples of Christ, today a dying liberal denomination.[1]

How true is this evaluation? In this chapter we will examine seven circumstances of the 1990's that seem to reflect the situation of the 1890's to see if we really are in the same boat. These matters include the instrumental music issue, women's public role in the church, the authority of elders, the rebaptism controversy, the "new hermeneutic," the increasing calls for division, and the push to force everyone into an exclusive camp.

First, however, we must lay a foundation for our study. Behind the specific controversies of the 1890's and the 1990's lie much deeper tensions that, while lying at the root of our current difficulties, have gone almost totally unnoticed. These tensions are the result of a fundamental shift now taking place in the worldview of American society.

A person's worldview comprises all the assumptions he or she has about the universe and how it operates. Worldview governs how people answer the question, "Why do things happen the way they do?" Most people are not conscious of their worldview. They have never tried to analyze the fundamental assumptions they have about how or why things happen. They take these beliefs for granted. Most people obtain their worldview from everything that surrounds them. What they read, see on television, hear on the radio, get in the classroom or from the pulpit--all these things shape people's understandings of the world, and most individuals are unaware of the process.

When circumstances begin to challenge the basic ways society understands the world, people become alarmed. They may come to believe that the very basis of order and existence is eroding. They are not sure what is happening—but are sure someone must be responsible for the disturbance. They strike out at enemies, real or imagined, that someone identifies as the source of the problem.

Examples of this abound in history. In the early 1800's in America, rapid changes in economic and social conditions made people very uncomfortable. They were experiencing what we know as the Industrial Revolution—a shift that changed almost every part of society—but all they knew was that things were not the way they used to be in "the good old days." Someone was taking away everything they valued, and they didn't know whom to blame. Demagogues—people who exploit the fears of others to gain power for themselves—targeted visible enemies for a confused and frightened public: paper money, public education, and licensing for doctors, among others.[2]

Worldview and Worldview Shifts

Changes in worldview for entire cultures or societies occur slowly through long and complicated processes. No one can pinpoint precisely when the Enlightenment worldview, for example, replaced medieval superstitious understandings. Over time, however, those Modern, or Enlightenment assumptions gradually pushed out the older understandings.

That shift, however, was enormously important. Under the medieval worldview, people understood the universe to operate by direct supernatural agency. If there was an eclipse of the sun or a plague, people believed God was punishing them for some terrible sin. They flocked to the churches to pray for forgiveness and restoration. Even if someone stumbled while walking down the path, it was supposed that a spirit, lurking on the side of the road, tripped the person. This was how people understood the world to operate. It was their worldview.

Slowly, because of events like Isaac Newton's scientific discoveries and John Locke's rational writings, people changed their worldview. They came to see the world not as controlled by unpredictable spiritual forces, but as orderly, operating according to natural laws discoverable by human reason. They came to believe that with their God-given reason, humans could reach true understandings of God, themselves and the universe. An eclipse or a plague or stumbling on the path were no longer seen as supernatural events, but simply the result of the natural laws of astronomy, biology and physics. They were all understood as perfectly natural happenings.

The Modern, or Enlightenment worldview was built on four basic ideas. The first is the ability of humans to progress, to move ever upward. People assumed that humans had the ability to solve all society's problems through science and technology. Eventually they came to believe that progress was inevitable—that humankind would continue to advance in every way. For many, this idea led to acceptance of biological evolution; that humans have evolved into the highest life forms and will continue to develop.

A second foundational idea of Enlightenment thought is the belief that the accumulation of scientific knowledge is inherently good. Such knowledge, people concluded, always promotes the progress of human society. This attitude, however, would eventually lead to the construction of weapons of mass destruction, developed through the scientific knowledge that was supposed to bring improvement to human existence.

Third, because modern thought placed such a high value on reason, many assumed that human reason alone would produce the most advanced societies and highest systems of morality. For the enlightened, there was no need for religion to impose morals. If properly educated, people would naturally arrive at right moral decisions on their own.

Fourth, the tendency of the modern worldview was to make God, as an explanation for anything, completely superfluous. Natural laws and processes supposedly explained everything. To be sure, not everyone stopped believing in God. But God was no longer a necessary part of the way they explained the day to day operation of the cosmos.[3]

The umbrella of modern Enlightenment thought had at its core faith in human reason, ability and progress. Of course, people have put those pieces together in different ways during the Modern era. Not everyone became a deist, denying any action of God in the world after creation. Many, in fact, used Enlightenment ideas to bolster Christianity.[4] Yet both the deists and the orthodox held these basic Modern assumptions in common.

Most of American society in the 1890's took for granted the ideas of progress and development, along with optimism about human goodness and ability. There was a significant shift going on in those years, however, that would shake the foundations of traditional Christianity. Influenced by European philosophers and theologians, the evolutionary ideas of Darwin, and the developmental ideas of the Biblical critics, some began to take Enlightenment ideas of human progress to their logical conclusion. Everything, they decided, was to be understood in terms of natural development—including religion and the Bible.

This conclusion is the essence of classical theological liberalism. The Bible and Christianity were seen as products of gradual evolution. God worked in the world only through natural processes of development. The worldview of the theological liberal emphasized human freedom and ability. They believed humans could eliminate evil and sin through Christian education.

The most significant happening of the 1890's, then, (with roots that go back several decades) was the shift in the minds of many Americans that led them to embrace an all-encompassing idea of progress and development—liberalism. Please note: this change was still under the larger umbrella of Enlightenment thought. As disruptive as theological liberalism was for many people, people who accepted it did not have to change their basic worldview. The changes all happened within the context of the Enlightenment or Modern worldview which included the ideas of progress, development, and human ability. Both the liberals and conservatives held the same basic assumptions about how the world worked. Liberal theologians merely took those ideas to their logical end.

Today another shift in thought is taking place. That fact is the most significant similarity between the 1890's and the 1990's. What is happening now, however, is in fundamental ways different from what happened in the 1890's.

An initial similarity is that, like the coming of the Enlightenment in the seventeenth century, ours is a shift of monumental proportions. But it is not simply a shifting of conclusions under the umbrella of the same basic assumptions, as was true in the development of theological liberalism in the 1890's.

Today, we are experiencing the breakup and rejection of the ideas that made up the Enlightenment worldview. This shift began at least as early as World War I, when the horrors of that destructive conflict deflated liberal optimism about the progress of human society. The Holocaust, World War II, and exploration of the inherently unpredictable world of quantum physics all served to further undermine the old liberal confidence in perpetual and orderly progress. Words being used to describe this new way of thinking are "Postmodern" and "post-Enlightenment." The terms are not well-defined, and some philosophers and theologians even deny the emergence of a new worldview.[5]

Regardless of how one chooses to describe it, more and more people no longer assume that humans can, with hard work and thought, solve all the world's problems. No longer do people scoff at the idea of the existence of a world beyond the physical senses. No longer are the evidences of God's work in the world explained away as coincidence.

The Postmodern worldview, like the Enlightenment worldview, is an umbrella that covers a multitude of positions, some contradictory. At its core, however, it negates the assumptions of the Enlightenment. Humans left alone with their reason do not create the highest codes of morality, Postmodernism declares. Rather, they create the most horribly evil systems imaginable, as evidenced by the case of Nazi morality. We are not on an inevitable advance, but seem bent on self-destruction. The science and technology that were to have solved all our problems have created new problems more troubling and resistant than the original ones. We have even produced devices capable of destroying all life on earth.

This new way of understanding constantly

pushes people toward the realization that there must be something beyond the the material and human. Otherwise, all is hopeless, terrifying, and ultimately futile. People are struggling to find a surety and hope beyond the material universe. Many are looking to Eastern religions, cults, or the so-called New Age movement. Christians know that the ultimate reality they seek is the God of the Bible (Acts 17:22-28).

The basic beliefs of the Modern worldview, taken to their logical end, worked against Christianity. Scientific modernism gutted Christianity's unique message, making it simply one religion among many. Theological liberalism weakened faith in the supernatural and authoritative nature of Scripture.

Certainly God's word was heard and obeyed, even under the umbrella of the Enlightenment worldview. Its ideas about human reason and ability spurred many to rigorous study of Scripture. The Stone-Campbell Restoration Movement began with that very motivation. Yet, despite Enlightenment assumptions about human ability to gain knowledge, people came to different understandings of Scripture, each party absolutely certain of its own interpretation. This attitude led to strife and division in countless instances.

The basic beliefs of the Postmodern worldview, in contrast, point people toward primary dependence on God and not their own abilities. God has revealed his will in Scripture. God's word is truth. In both the Old and New Testaments he has shown what he wants from us, yet we have a very hard time understanding it. Briefly, he wants us to have a relationship of love with him that results in a relationship of love with each other (Deuteronomy 6:5; Leviticus 19:18; Matthew 22:36-40; 1 Corinthians 13). Only

Christians have this message, and it is the only message that can truly satisfy the longings of "Postmodern" people.

From the 1890's to Today: a Comparison

With that discussion as background, we are ready to look at seven points of tension in Churches of Christ to see how our situation today compares with that of a century ago.

1. Instrumental Music in Worship The nineteenth-century struggles over instrumental music in worship greatly affected Churches of Christ. Both sides used the forms of logic and argumentation characteristic of the Enlightenment era. In the many debates, whether opponents wielded the sword of logic in written or oral form, those defending each position were fully convinced of the correctness of their conclusions in the end. The non-use of instruments by Churches of Christ became a mark of our identity, symbolizing important stands we took about biblical authority and the nature of worship.

Today the issue is hot again. The topic has generated over two hundred articles and speeches in major journals and lectureships during the last fifteen years, as well as a book on the controversy's history and a forum at Freed-Hardeman University in 1991.[6] The most recent flurry of articles is partly a reaction to the Restoration Forum meetings with members of the Independent Christian Churches and the increased fellowship with that communion in several parts of the country.

Never in our history has this issue been dormant. The *Gospel Advocate Index* lists articles on the topic for practically every year from 1855 to 1982.

Until recently, however, it was taken for granted that no leader in Churches of Christ would openly question our opposition to the instrument's use.

In the 1890's the question of the use of instrumental music marked a visible dividing line between the progressive or liberal part of the Restoration Movement and the conservative Churches of Christ. While more than simply a liberal-conservative split,[7] the adoption of the instrument was definitely compatible with the liberal notions of progress and development. It was an improvement, an advance, in the eyes of many.

In the 1990's the instrumental music matter, as it always has, stands for something more basic. For many, our position on the instrument has become a symbol of everything Churches of Christ have stood for through the years. They strongly defend our position with the arguments hammered out during the earlier struggle. The fact that fewer and fewer people settle for the arguments and answers of a century ago is frustrating and puzzling to those who propound them.

We must understand this conflict, like the others, in light of the worldview change now taking place. Those willing to reexamine our traditional position on instrumental music, who perhaps question the all-important status we have given it, are not theological liberals who reject the authority of Scripture. Instead, they are deeply committed to conservative belief about the Bible and its nature; its full inspiration and authority. They do not, however, put as much faith in the inferential process necessary to reach our traditional conclusions about the use of instruments. People living in a Postmodern world no longer approach every question with the assumptions of the Enlightenment era. They simply have less confidence in the intricate logical arguments of the last century and may even be repelled by the self-satisfied, arrogant attitudes that too often accompanied the conclusions reached with those arguments.

There are some who seem to think that by introducing instrumental music into worship they can improve the public's perception of Churches of Christ as a narrow legalistic sect. They are willing to risk disruption of the body for the sake of a forced identity change. Unquestionably, this is a problem. Yet not even these people are approaching Scripture with theologically liberal notions. Theological liberals would have little interest in what the Bible says on such a matter. All sides in our context are vitally interested in what an authoritative Bible says or does not say about it.

2. Women's Roles The role of women in the church was a focus of controversy in the late 1800's, just as it is today. The exchanges between David Lipscomb and Silena Holman in the *Gospel Advocate* are typical. Holman, the wife of an elder of the church in Fayetteville, Tennessee, pointed out passages in both the Old and New Testaments that showed women exercising public roles. She agreed with Lipscomb that man is head of the woman and that woman's primary focus is the home. Yet she insisted that this did not absolutely remove women from public leadership roles. She rejected the distinction made between what women can do in public and private spheres.

Suppose a dozen men and women were in my parlor and I talked to them of the gospel and exhorted them to obey it? Exactly how many would have to be added to the number to make my talk and exhortation a public instead of a private one?

I believe that a learned Christian woman may expound the scriptures and urge obedience to them to one hundred men and women at one time, as well as to one hundred, one at a time, and do much good, and no more violate a scriptural command in one instance than the other.[8]

Though Lipscomb published Holman's articles, he absolutely disagreed with her, and often said so. He saw the changing role of women, *including their campaign for the right to vote,* as pure infidelity to Scripture. At the meeting of the American Christian Missionary Society in Nashville in 1892, Lipscomb was appalled to see women addressing the assembly. He concluded that the entire tone of the meeting showed that those Disciples had rejected God and set aside the authority of his word.[9]

The women's movement, along with a liberal developmental view of Scripture and society, affected the way people understood women's roles in the 1890's. In our own day the feminist movement has influenced society's attitudes about women's roles. Our own journals and lectureships have generated well over three hundred articles and speeches, as well as several books concerning women in church work during the past two decades. But this question among Churches of Christ today is not merely a resurrection of the theologically liberal and conservative positions of a century ago.

In today's larger American evangelical world, understandings of women's roles sharply divide biblical conservatives. Two organizations represent this bifurcation. On one hand, The Council on Biblical

Manhood and Womanhood holds a traditional view, rejecting roles such as preacher and elder for women. On the other hand, Christians for Biblical Equality promotes full and equal ministry roles for men and women. Both claim full allegiance to the inspiration and authority of Scripture. Both reject theologically liberal assumptions. Both insist that their conclusions are solidly based in Scripture.[10]

In this issue we can see, perhaps more clearly than in any other, that the tensions most affecting our congregations are between conservatives and conservatives—not between liberals and conservatives. In other words, this and the other areas of conflict are between groups that all hold to the unique inspiration and authority of Scripture. True theological liberals have long since moved beyond concern about whether apparent biblical restrictions on women have *any* relevance for today's "enlightened" church. They would view this argument as so much beating of a long-dead horse.

This issue will become more important for us as the decade progresses. No one today, whatever their philosophical or theological positions, holds all the old nineteenth-century assumptions of woman's place. Lipscomb and many of his day assumed that women are intellectually inferior because of their emotional nature; that they are not fit to participate in the political process; and that, significantly, they are spiritually superior to men. Much of that package of ideas was the product of American culture, not biblical truth. There is already an extensive probing into this question among us, and none of the assumptions of the past will be exempt from scrutiny. But the discussion in Churches of Christ is and will continue to be rooted in Scripture.

3. The Authority of Elders The authority of elders was a prominent issue in the late 1800's, influenced heavily by what historian Alan Trachtenberg called "the incorporation of America."[11] American society bought into the ideals of centralized control of business, of organization and efficiency, obedience and loyalty. Inevitably, these ideas affected the churches of the country as well. In the larger Restoration Movement, centralized control grew through the various societies already in place. But even in the churches that rejected the societies, elderships were structured to wield power in the same manner that boards of directors control business operations.

Some, like David Lipscomb and E. G. Sewell, resisted this understanding of church leadership. They insisted that the notion of "office" in the church did not mean a position that conferred power as it did in the world. Lipscomb wrote:

> All the authority [elders] possess in any matter is the moral weight their wisdom and devotion carry with them, gained through obedience to the will of God, and the express declaration that they and all of God's servants must be respected in doing the works assigned them by the Holy Spirit.[12]

> Whenever a man or set of men . . . assume to exercise authority in a church by virtue of some official appointment, or to assert they have rights and authority as officers above others and assume to exert their rights, without the full consent and approval of the members, they should be resisted even to the disruption of the body. . . . Whenever a man in the church of Christ claims authority or exercises power merely on official grounds, he is as essentially a pope and claims the prerogative of papacy as fully as does he of Rome.[13]

Despite Lipscomb's and Sewell's strong re-sistance, the corporate business model became the norm in most churches. Elders were officers with power to make decisions, handle finances, perpetuate the eldership, and demand loyalty and obedience. The nineteenth-century corporate model grew out of the liberal notions of an ever-developing, ever more effi-cient society.

Surprisingly, over seven hundred articles deal-ing with elders have appeared in our journals during the last twenty years. Most deal in one way or an-other with the elders' authority. Just as in the late nineteenth century, there are some who saw the role of elder as an *office* endowed with *authority.* Increas-ingly, however, others are rejecting the notion of authority to describe the nature of elders' leadership.[14]

In 1985, the Gospel Advocate Company pub-lished a book by Jack P. Lewis titled *Leadership Ques-tions Confronting the Church.* In chapter four, titled "Greek Words for Elders," Lewis surveyed every Greek word in the New Testament that was used for elders and their function. He concluded that in no passage is there any connection of the idea of "au-thority" to the eldership.

> . . . all the Greek terms, when considered from the viewpoint of how the elder should conceive of him-self, stress images of sacrifice and service rather than images of authority. . . . If one may state what appears a paradox, the elder should conceive of himself, not in terms of authority, but in terms of "doing a good work"; while the congregation should relate to him as God's steward.[15]

Today, those arguing against the traditional understanding of the authority of elders are not necessarily Postmodern in their assumptions, any more than Lipscomb or Harding were. Yet people who live in a Postmodern world, who do not see the Bible through the lenses of the Enlightenment era, are questioning older authoritarian assumptions concerning the nature of church leadership. This is the case not because they are theological liberals—but precisely because they are *not*.

4. The Re-baptism Controversy　　Another heated controversy of the 1890's involved the question of re-baptism. It centered on the conflict between David Lipscomb, editor of the *Gospel Advocate,* and Austin McGary, editor of the *Firm Foundation*. McGary started his paper in 1884 to combat what he viewed as Lipscomb's acceptance of "Baptist baptism," or "sect baptism." Lipscomb taught that if a person believed in Christ, repented of sins, and, desiring to obey God, was immersed, that person was added to the church. It made no difference where or by whom the baptism was performed as long as those scriptural components were present.[16]

McGary countered that without prior and clear knowledge that in the act of baptism one received forgiveness of sins, it could not be scriptural. Lipscomb answered that certainly, sins were remitted in baptism, but that there were other designs for the act too, the main one being to put people into Christ. Lipscomb further insisted that baptism to join a certain church, whether it was called "Baptist Church" or "Church of Christ," was not scriptural.[17]

Eventually, the strict position taught by McGary became dominant in Churches of Christ. Strong advocates of it require "re-baptism" of anyone not baptized by one of us, which would presumably assure the proper understanding at the time of the immersion.[18] Increasingly, this position is being challenged as sectarian.[19] Again, it is not a question of "liberal versus conservative." No one involved in this discussion denies that baptism is essential for salvation. Nor do all those who question the strict position reflect Postmodern ideas. The "Lipscomb view," however, reflected his emphasis on God's work and not on perfect intellectual understandings by the person baptized. This attitude is definitely compatible with a Postmodern worldview.

5. *Hermeneutics* An extremely important point of tension surrounds what has become known as "the new hermeneutic." Here, the words simply mean a new way of understanding or interpreting the Bible. The controversy has become so heated that to label someone a proponent of the new hermeneutic is in some circles the same as saying the person rejects the authority of Scripture, is an infidel and should be cut off from fellowship. Why does a discussion of how to understand the Bible evoke such violent reactions?

According to some, our old approach to Scripture gave relevance only to divine commands, apostolic examples, and necessary inferences in the New Testament.[20] By extracting and piecing together these items, the argument runs, we will have knowledge of all God wants us to know and do. The Old Testament was relegated to secondary status at best.

Whether or not this is an accurate description of how we have approached Scripture, those who are exploring other approaches are not offering "liberal" alternatives. The theological liberals of the late nineteenth century held an evolutionary view of

Scripture. The Bible, they believed, was produced through natural human processes which moved from primitive notions about God and the universe to more refined and sophisticated ideas. Furthermore, this process of advance has continued, they stated. The superstitious notions found even in the New Testament writers, they said, had to be brought into the modern world and reinterpreted according to modern, more sophisticated understandings. The Scriptures were to be understood as a record of God's past dealings with people as perceived by the primitive writers and compilers. Their authority was not to be understood in any literal way, according to this view.

Those probing the matter of hermeneutics in Churches of Christ today are not possessed of such notions. They believe in the unique inspiration and full authority of Scripture, which is precisely the reason they question what they see as a limiting and misdirected approach to understanding the Bible. They do not deny the importance of obeying direct commands, recognizing apostolic examples or grappling with what statements of Scripture lead us to conclude. Instead, they are saying that if these are the only criteria for deciding what is relevant in Scripture, something is wrong, because that approach focuses on *human* ability to obey, recognize and reason.

At its worst, a command-example-inference hermeneutic sees the New Testament as an unassembled puzzle with extra pieces. With our reason we must extract the essential pieces and construct the list of things we must do to define our lives before God. While the contention that Churches of Christ have rigidly and exclusively adhered to such a hermeneutic in the past seems to be a straw man, those pushing for something different insist that the focus of our approach to Scripture should be on God and his wondrous and gracious work for us, not on our actions. They are every bit as serious about understanding what God intends from Scripture as any who reject the need for a new or renewed hermeneutic. Those who call for an approach to Scripture that focuses on God and his work rather than on human achievement, who refuse to make binding judgments concerning issues the Bible itself does not address, are not theological liberals in any legitimate sense of the word.

6. Calls for Separation (Sand Creek) Our present decade resembles the 1890's in the rising call for division in Churches of Christ. Perhaps the most celebrated calls for separation in the 19th century came in 1889 and 1892. In those years, several churches in Illinois called for an open break with those they believed had left biblical truth for "modern fads and foolishness." The "Sand Creek Address and Declaration" condemned

> . . . unlawful methods resorted to in order to raise or get money for religious purposes. . . the use of instrumental music in the worship and the select choir to the virtual if not the real abandonment of congregational singing. Likewise the man-made society for mission work and the one-man imported preacher pastor to feed and watch over the flock. These with many other objectionable and unauthorized things are now taught and practiced in many of the congregations. . . .

The document concluded,

> . . . we are impelled from a sense of duty to say that all such as are guilty of teaching or allowing

and practicing the many innovations and corruptions to which we have referred, after having had sufficient time for meditation and reflection, if they will not turn away from such abominations, that we cannot and will not regard them as brethren.[21]

On the other side, J. H. Garrison, editor of the *Christian-Evangelist* and a "progressive," asserted that such divisive attitudes were surely held only by "a few misguided brethren."

As long as there is any considerable part of our membership whose conception of Christianity is such that the adoption of any expedient for the furtherance of Christian work, or as an accessory to Christian worship, wounds their conscience, because not specifically authorized in the Scripture, these congregational strifes will continue.[22]

Later, Garrison chided,

What is the use of any religious body talking about Christian unity on a broad scale for the whole religious world, while it is divided on questions of Tweedledee and Tweedledum?[23]

Statements are being issued today which are reminiscent of the Sand Creek Address and Declaration and Garrison's contentions. In late 1986, a widely circulated "Expression of Concern," spoke against what it labeled "the liberalism that is so evident in the brotherhood today." Though not calling for an open break, it warned of

. . . a drifting from the Bible-centered, definitive, distinctive doctrine that once characterized our preaching. Presently uncertain sounds and weak messages emanate from many pulpits among us. Brethren are becoming accustomed to diluted and polluted preaching.

The statement accused some of trying to restructure the worship, organization, and work of the church and of harboring a spirit of doctrinal compromise, allowing the church to be influenced by the world rather than the world by the church. The document gives no specific examples of these accusations, but in a second section it attacks Abilene Christian University for harboring teachers who taught evolution as fact.

Others have been more strident. In his August 1986 editorial, Ira Rice asked,

> What is it going to take for these false teachers and us to get out of each other's hair? Must we have another census? They don't dare debate their cause—so that's out! Some say that all we can do is just keep on preaching and teaching the word, contending for the faith—and we surely can do that. But why prolong the misery? Why not just come out from among them and be separate, like 2 Corinthians 6 says![24]

The previous year, Jerry Moffitt wrote these words in an article titled "The Current Digression Among Us:" "Let's close the ranks, brandish the sword, stand up and speak out. . . we are assured of victory. Join the fray."[25] In 1993 John M. Brown of Flatwoods, Kentucky, urged those whom he felt were no longer teaching what Churches of Christ have always taught to "Hurry up and get on out! Please disassociate yourself with churches of Christ; start your own Community Church. Just leave us alone!"[26]

Though the strongest calls for division appear to be coming from extreme traditionalists opposed to any modification of established beliefs and practices, there are frustrated voices from other positions, just as in the 1890's. Rubel Shelly, one of the most influential of the "progressive" leaders, characterized traditionalists as "hard-liners" who "subvert productive energy," using intimidation to gain power. Nostalgic for the conditions of the 1950's, this "extreme right" group, he says, slanders its enemies and plays on the fears of those it wants to control.

> Just as the Mafia gets away with many of its crimes by intimidating people, so do other evil people do their sorry work by harassment and threat. Attempting to ruin people is their sport. And some have proved themselves to be gold-medal caliber at it. Their time is passing rapidly. People are sick of it and will no longer be threatened by them. Their attacks only tend to build credibility for their targets. People aren't as shallow as some speakers and writers suppose.[27]

Some sharing similar views have left Churches of Christ in frustration at our failure to make immediate changes they deemed necessary.[28]

Calls for division are increasing in the 1990's, just as they did in the nineteenth century. Traditionalists identify "liberalism" as the enemy. Those anxious for change see the foes as sectarianism and rationalism. The temptation to act out of anger and mistrust is increasing at both ends of the spectrum.

7. The Push to Force Everyone to Take Sides
The spirit of division always presses people to side with some brothers and sisters to the exclusion of others. In an 1897 "open letter," one of T. B. Larimore's former pupils challenged the beloved evangelist to declare himself on the issues then troubling the movement. Larimore realized what the real question was.

> To which—or *what*—party do *I* belong in this unfortunate controversy? "That's the question." Had I "spoken out" on "matters" mentioned in your "open

letter," this question had never arisen; for *all* had known. Your letter is proof positive, then, that you and . . . THOUSANDS of other friends before whom "my life is an open book" believe I have never "spoken out," have never expressed an opinion or a preference—on ANY of these things . . . over which brethren are wrangling and disputing and dividing the church of Christ— NEVER.

My dear brother, if you deem it possible to believe it possible for a man to be *in no sense* a partisan, but just simply and solely a Christian, in this intensely partisan age, please *try* to believe that I am not a partisan. . . .

As to the matter of fellowship, Larimore expressed his strong feelings this way:

When Bro. Campbell took my confession, on my twenty-first birthday, he questioned me relative to *none* of these "matters now retarding the progress of the cause of Christ." While thousands have stood before me, hand in mine, and made "the good confession," I have never questioned *one* of them about these "matters." Shall I now renounce and disfellowship all of these who do not understand these things exactly as *I* understand them? They may refuse to recognize or fellowship or affiliate with ME; but I will NEVER refuse to recognize or fellowship or affiliate with them-- NEVER.[29]

These troubling issues of the late 1800's are again in the forefront. But the situation today is fundamentally different. Beneath the surface similarities, there are very different ways of understanding reality. Christians in the Postmodern world, in the best sense of that complex term, insist that the key is faithfulness to the God of Scripture and to his power to lead, rather than confidence in human ability to get everything right. Christians in the Postmodern world must not avoid approaching the Scriptures with scholarly tools of study. They must fully utilize their God-given reason to reach correct conclusions about truth. But they should do so with the realization that they will never reach true understanding of God's Word merely by using technical tools.

This is not merely a matter of semantics. Theological liberalism undermined belief in the unique supernatural inspiration and authority of Scripture. The Postmodern worldview rejects the very premises of the Modern liberal theological views. Our struggle, then, in the Churches of Christ is not between liberals and conservatives; it is between Modern conservatives and Postmodern conservatives. [For a graphic representation of the spectrum of conservative theological thought, see the chart at the end of this chapter.]

Postmodernism has aspects that are potentially as anti-Christian as some views of Modern thought. But the essential elements of this worldview relentlessly prod secularized, materialistic people toward belief in a higher power. These ideas thrust upon such people the realization that they are not in charge of the universe.

We ought not to fear the move into the Postmodern world. In any case, we cannot stop it. We can refuse to recognize the changes, and we can misunderstand and criticize what is happening. But we cannot stop it any more than medieval church leaders could stop the Age of Enlightenment by forcing Galileo to recant his assertion that the earth was not the center of the universe.

The gospel is true and relevant and powerful, whatever the pervasive thought patterns of an era. People can be brought into a proper relationship with God through the directives of his word in the context of any worldview, using that worldview's own basic premises. May God help us, as members of his family, to be able to tell the good news of his salvation to the Postmodern world we are now entering.

The point of this chapter is not that the differences among us can be resolved simply by understanding that there is a new worldview emerging. The differences are real and have theological significance. They are not, however, differences between one group that is trying to be faithful to Scripture and another that places little value on scriptural authority. Simply understanding the worldview differences will not solve the problems or cause strife to cease. That will only happen if we submit to God's plan for maintaining unity.

Endnotes

[1] See for example Howard Winters, "The Restoration and Liberalism," *Firm Foundation* 93 (September 21, 1976):599; and Bill Hamrick, "Is History Repeating Itself?" *Christian Worker* 71 (March 1, 1985):2.

[2] See Robert V. Remini, *Andrew Jackson and the Course of American Democracy, 1833-1845* (New York: Harper & Row, Publishers, 1984).

[3] Diogenes Allen, *Christian Belief in a Postmodern World* (Louisville: Westminster/John Knox Press, 1989), 2-5.

[4] See especially Joseph Butler, *The Analogy of Religion, Natural and Revealed, to the Constitution and Course of Nature*, first published in 1736, and William Paley, *A View of the Evidences of Christianity*, first published in 1794.

[5] Skepticism about human reason is not new.

David Hume, Immanuel Kant, and Friederich Schleiermacher, among others, all lived in the "modern" age yet tried to destroy naive or arrogant confidence in human knowledge.

[6] Julian Ernest Choate and William Woodson, *Sounding Brass and Clanging Symbols: The History and Significance of Instrumental Music in the Restoration Movement, 1827-1968* (Henderson, TN: Freed Hardeman University, 1990).

[7] See for example David Edwin Harrell, Jr., *Quest for a Christian America: The Disciples of Christ and American Society to 1866* (Nashville: The Disciples of Christ Historical Society, 1966), 67-68.

[8] Silena Holman, "Let Your Women Keep Silent," *Gospel Advocate* 30 (August 1, 1888): 8; "Woman's Scriptural Status Again," *Gospel Advocate* 30 (November 21, 1888): 8-9.

[9] David Lipscomb, "Convention Thoughts," *Gospel Advocate* 34 (November 10, 1892):709.

[10] See for example John Piper and Wayne Grudem, eds., *Recovering Biblical Manhood and Womanhood: A Response to Evangelical Feminism* (Wheaton, IL: Council on Biblical Manhood and Womanhood, 1991); Richard and Catherine Kroeger, *I Suffer Not a Woman: Rethinking I Timothy 2:11-15 in Light of Ancient Evidence* (Grand Rapids, MI: Baker Book House, 1992); and Charles Trombley, *Who Said Women Can't Teach?* (Bridge Publishing Company, 1985).

[11] Alan Trachtenberg, *The Incorporation of America: Culture and Society in the Gilded Age* (New York: Hill and Wang, 1982).

[12] David Lipscomb, "Officers and Officialism in the Church of God," *Gospel Advocate* 9 (July 18, 1867):568.

[13] David Lipscomb, "Church Authority," *Gospel Advocate* 19 (April 12, 1877):232.

[14] See Tim Willis, "The Office of Elder in Church of Christ Publications, 1950-1980," Paper presented at the Christian Scholars Conference, David Lipscomb University, July 20, 1991.

[15] Jack P. Lewis, *Leadership Questions Confronting the Church* (Nashville: Christian Communications, 1985), 34.

[16] David Lipscomb, "What Constitutes Valid Baptism," *Gospel Advocate* 15 (January 9, 1873):41-43.

[17] See discussion in Robert E. Hooper, *Crying in the Wilderness: A Biography of David Lipscomb* (Nashville: David Lipscomb College, 1979):194-195, 210-213.

[18] See Charles L. Houser, "Should Baptists Be Rebaptized?" *Firm Foundation* 103 (June 10, 1986):359-360; Jule L. Miller, "Helping 'Baptized' People to be Scripturally Baptized," *Gospel Advocate* 134 (June 1992):27-29.

[19] See for example Jimmy Allen, *Re-Baptism: What One Must Know to be Born Again* (West Monroe, LA: Howard Publishing Co., 1991).

[20] Thomas Campbell in proposition six of the "Declaration and Address of the Christian Association" rejected requiring inferences for extending full Christian fellowship.

[21] P. P. Warren, "Sand Creek Address and Declaration," *Christian Leader* 3 (September 10, 1889):2.

[22] J. H. Garrison, "Mark Those Who Cause Divisions," *Christian-Evangelist* 25 (November 29, 1888):739.

[23] "Unity Like Charity Should Begin at Home,"

The Christian-Evangelist 41 (May 12, 1904):597.

[24] Ira Y. Rice, Jr., "What Will it Take for Faithful to 'Come Out' and 'Be Separate'?" *Contending for the Faith* 17 (August 1986):2.

[25] Jerry Moffitt, "The Current Digression Among Us," *Contending for the Faith* 16(October 1985):5;see also Danny Bennett, "Strangers," *Contending for the Faith* 21(July 1990):12.

[26] John M. Brown, "Hurry Up and Get Out," *Hammer & Tongs* 2 (November-December 1993):1.

[27] Rubel Shelly, "The Sport of 'Ruining People,'" *Love Lines: The Weekly Bulletin of the Family of God at Woodmont Hills* 19 (August 19, 1993):3; "Right-Wing Coups," quoted in James W. Boyd, "Shelly on Right-Wing Coups," *Contending for the Faith* 23 (October 1992):1.

[28] Randy Mayeux, most recently minister for the Preston Road Church of Christ in Dallas, and Bill Swetmon, formerly of Pittman Creek Church of Christ near Dallas, are among those who have have left to lead "non-denominational" churches where instrumental music could be used and where they could minister to the "unchurched" according to their own convictions.

[29] T. B. Larimore, "Reply to O. P. Spiegel's Open Letter," *Christian Standard* 33 (July 24, 1897), 965-967.

CHART: TYPES OF CONSERVATIVES

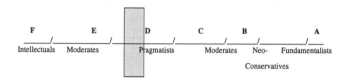

POSTMODERN CONSERVATIVES

MODERN CONSERVATIVES

F   E   D   C   B   A

Intellectuals   Moderates   Pragmatists   Moderates   Neo-   Fundamentalists

Conservatives

A. Fundamentalists

--Aggressive and often abrasive traditionalists.

--Unswervingly loyal to traditional conclusions and methods of reasoning.

--Fervently believe their conclusions are the truth of Scripture; reject any method of study that could arrive at alternate conclusions.

--Thoroughly rational in approach to Scripture and truth.

--Often label all other positions as "liberal."

B. Neo-Conservatives

--Reactionary; fearful of irrational or non-rational tendencies perceived among pietists and postmoderns, often without making distinctions between these two differing positions.

--Usually highly educated

--Incompatible with fundamentalists, but can be quite aggressive in condemning departures from traditional theology and stances.

C. Modern Conservative Moderates

--Fear moves toward apostasy by pietists and postmoderns, not distinguishing between the two.

--Rejected by fundamentalists as "too soft."

--Less reactionary than categories A and B, though becoming more alarmed at turmoil and division.

--Sometimes deny or minimize Restoration/ Church of Christ heritage.

--Emphasize practical matters, including evangelism.

--Still thoroughly "Modern" in worldview.

D. Pragmatists

--Committed to relevance of faith to contemporary culture; sometimes appearing totally "market-driven" in their acceptance of charismatic manifestations, instrumental music, new worship styles, and other current trends.

--More in touch with broad evangelical religious spectrum than with fellowship of Churches of Christ, though some have great interest in promoting spiritual renewal, as they understand it, among our churches.

E. Postmodern Conservative Moderates

--Strongly skeptical toward infallibility of human rational processes, though not rejecting rational thought.

--Some are pietistic or apocalyptic, but generally characterized by deep commitment to biblical authority and spirituality.

F. Intellectual Postmoderns

--Tend toward the pessimism characteristic of much Postmodern thought.

--Pensive, philosophical, theological.

--Vitally concerned with humanity's right relationship to God.

Will the Cycle be Unbroken?

Chapter 7

God's Prescription for Unity

A letter to the editor of one of our papers expressed alarm at the statement of a friend that it looked like division among the Churches of Christ was unavoidable. The editor of the paper replied:

> If a people pleading for the union of all Christians cannot maintain the unity of the Spirit in the bond of peace in their own limited communion, and peaceably dispose of all questions . . . then this plea for union [is] as riduculous a farce as was ever played before the public. The Apostolic churches had much graver errors in doctrine and practice to dispose of than any that are troubling us; and many had a strong propensity to file off into parties. The lessons of Christian liberty, of tolerance and forbearance, of patience and gentleness taught by the apostles, need to be carefully attended to. No one should allow himself to indulge such fears or to utter them. As long as we are one in the faith of Christ and in acknowledging his authority, we will remain one people; and free and kindly discussion will bring us out of all our differences.[1]

The year was 1869, and the editor was Isaac

Errett of the *Christian Standard.* We know painfully well that the Restoration movement did not hold together. Indeed, to some of the churches in our movement, Errett has become one of the villains in the division, despite his intense efforts to mediate between the contending groups and to prevent the split that was finally realized in the 1890's.

A century later, we in Churches of Christ again face the alarming prospect of division. This time a better word might be splintering, for there are many groups that seem to be pulling off in different directions.

Is there hope of avoiding a fracturing of Churches of Christ, a weakening of our efforts to be New Testament Christians and the kind of people God would have us be? Looking at history or sociology, there doesn't seem to be much reason for hope. It appears that human beings are going to act in ways that are willful and full of pride—in ways that inevitably cause division, even among those trying to do God's will.

However, when we look to the Scriptures we have hope. Their message is that we don't have to be pulled into the ways of the world. The power of God can change our lives, can make them more and more like the perfect human life—our example, Jesus Christ. In this chapter we will focus on what I believe is the key to hope for avoiding this tragedy of division. This key is centered in the message of Philippians 2:5.

Context of Philippians 2:5

Many regard Paul's letter to Philippi as the most intimate and personal of all his writings. He had established this church in the region of Macedonia, and the Philippians had financially supported him several times. Most recently they had sent one of their own to Paul in the person of Epaphroditus, who brought money to the imprisoned apostle, evidently in Rome. Epaphroditus had become deathly ill while with Paul, but was now recovered enough to take this letter back to the Philippian church.

In this letter, Paul deals with the Philippians' problems gently and even indirectly. Yet it is obvious from a careful reading that the Philippian church had a problem with fractiousness and division. In three of the book's four chapters Paul gently urges them as a congregation—and in 4:2 urges individuals—to be united, in harmony with one another, and especially to be humble of mind.

The key verses appear in the section where Paul gives the ultimate example of humility to the Philippians. Older translations such as the King James and Revised Standard say, "Have this mind within you. . ." We can see the meaning in contemporary language in the New American Standard and New International versions: "Have this attitude in yourselves, which was also in Christ Jesus." We are to have the same attitude that Jesus had.

The immediate context for that statement is found in 1:27 through 2:8 (quotations from the NIV):

> Whatever happens, conduct yourselves in a manner worthy of the gospel of Christ. Then, whenever I come and see you or only hear about you in my absence, I will know that you stand firm in one spirit, contending as one person for the faith of the gospel without being frightened in any way by those who oppose you. This is a sign to them that they will be destroyed, but that you will be saved—and that by God.
>
> For it has been granted to you on behalf of Christ not only to believe on him, but also to suffer for

him, since you are going through the same struggle you saw I had, and now hear that I still have.

If you have any encouragement from being united with Christ, if any comfort from his love, if any fellowship with the Spirit, if any tenderness and compassion, then make my joy complete by being like-minded, having the same love, being one in spirit and purpose.

Do nothing out of selfish ambition or vain conceit, but in humility consider others better than yourselves. Each of you should look not only to your own interests, but also to the interests of others.

Your attitude should be the same as that of Christ Jesus:

Who being in very nature God,
did not consider equality with God something
to be grasped (held on to),
but made himself nothing, taking the very
nature of a servant,
being made in human likeness,
and being found in appearance as a man, he
humbled himself
and became obedient to the point of death,
even death on a cross!

What Kind of Attitude Did Jesus Have?

In verse 27 Paul tells the Philippians to act as citizens of heaven ought to act, namely to live in harmony and unity with their fellow saints. In 2:1-4 he gives four reasons to live in unity and explains in more detail precisely what that means. Finally he gives the ultimate example that provides the underlying attitude necessary for living in unity. That attitude, embodied in the life of Jesus Christ, is characterized by humility and self-denial, and we are told to have that mind. H. Leo Boles, in an article entitled "The Mind of Christ," stated:

The mind of Christ is the humility of Christ. The real test of discipleship with Christ is revealed in the humility or lack of humility in our lives. The more intimate we become with Christ the more meekness and lowliness of heart will be manifested in our lives.[2]

134

There are other texts that illustrate the mind or attitude of Christ. One is 1 Peter 2:21-23:

> Christ suffered for you, leaving you an example, that you should follow in his steps. He committed no sin, and no deceit was found in his mouth. When they hurled insults at him, he did not retaliate; when he suffered, he made no threats. Instead, he entrusted himself to him who judges justly.

Another is 1 John 3:16: "This is how we know what love is: Jesus Christ laid down his life for us. And we ought to lay down our lives for our brothers."

These and other such passages elaborate on Christ's fundamental attitude of humility. Christians with a combative spirit, perhaps to justify their own actions, have sometimes tried to correct what they fear are misunderstandings of humility. The editor of a Chattanooga paper, *The Examiner*, sharply reprimanded one reader for portraying Christ as ". . . a first-class wimp, who went about spouting little sweet talk to please everybody." Some respond to admonitions to humility by saying, "Jesus was sometimes harsh!" These statements reflect a notion about Jesus that appears to contradict the Scriptures' emphasis on his essential humility.

Was Jesus Ever Angry or Harsh?

Those whose work is filled with attacks on brothers and sisters often justify their actions by pointing to instances in scripture when Jesus became angry and harsh. However, in every one of the five or so situations in the New Testament that refer to Jesus becoming angry or using harsh words for people, his ire is directed toward Jewish religious officials or his own disciples. In other words, Jesus' anger was always directed toward people who should have known the fundamental importance of humility, love, mercy and compassion, but who got things mixed up. He upbraided them because they didn't understand the real bottom line of true religion.

Matthew 21:12-13 and the parallel passages in Mark 11, Luke 19, and John 2 are perhaps the most noted examples of Jesus acting in a harsh manner. You know the story well. Jesus entered the temple area after his triumphal entry into Jerusalem and began driving out the people who were buying and selling there. He also turned over the tables being used by the money changers and the dove sellers, refusing to allow anyone to pass through the temple courts with any kind of merchandise. This is probably the instance most frequently used to justify harsh words and actions against brothers or sisters who believe or practice something deemed unscriptural by their antagonists. But does it really serve such a purpose? There are some serious cautions to using these passages in that way.

First, Jesus had the authority to take this drastic action. In a unique sense, this was his Father's house. We do not have the authority or right to take matters into our hands in this manner, particularly in light of the overwhelming scriptural admonitions we will examine shortly that point away from such actions. Second, Jesus' actions were directed against a religious custom that had become accepted and taken for granted by the religious establishment of his day. The exchange and sales system provided a sanctioned method for the people to pay the temple tax and purchase proper animals for sacrifice. These were accepted traditions, expedient ways of carrying out God's commands of sacrifice that were sanctioned and approved by the leaders. If this passage can be used to justify attacking anyone, it would seem to be directed against established religious traditions (good, bad or neutral) that have the time-accepted approval of religious leaders.

As the first of several corollary examples, look at Mark 3:1-6. Jesus' enemies were waiting to see if he would heal a man with a shriveled hand on the Sabbath. When Jesus asked them whether it was lawful to do good or evil on the Sabbath, they all kept their mouths shut. In verse 5, Jesus looks at them in anger, deeply distressed at their stubborn hearts. They did not care about the man in need. They had no compassion—and Jesus healed the man boldly in their presence.

In Mark 10:13-16 Jesus became indignant at his disciples because they rebuked the people who were bringing their little children to him. The disciples were more concerned with appearance and procedure than with the simplicity and love exemplified by these little ones.

In Luke 9:51-56, when the people of a Samaritan village had refused to help the Lord's disciples, James and John asked Jesus if they should call down fire from heaven to destroy the village. Jesus, the passage says, rebuked James and John, and they went on to another village. The two brothers were zealous for Jesus. After all, these people had rejected their master! They were void, however, of what was most important in followers of the Lord: compassion and humility.

Finally, in a number of places, including

Matthew chapters 15 and 23 and Luke 3:7, Jesus has harsh words for the chief religious leaders of his day—the teachers of the law and the Pharisees. His condemnations were directed primarily against their legalism and hypocrisy. In Matthew 15 Jesus applies a description from Isaiah to them: "These people honor me with their lips, but their hearts are far from me. They worship me in vain; their teachings are but rules taught by men." These leaders were incapable of true spiritual self-examination.

In Matthew 23 Jesus sharply criticizes the scribes and Pharisees for meticulously keeping even the minute parts of the Law, and even for their efforts at converting non-Jews. What could be wrong with these actions? They were condemned because they neglected the weightier matters—justice, mercy, and faithfulness. They were condemned because of what was in their hearts. Jesus could know exactly what was on the inside—what their minds or attitudes really were.

There is no justification in these passages for attacking sincere brothers and sisters. The attitude of Christ that we are told to model is characterized by humility and compassion. That is in no way negated by the passages just examined.

Attitude is All-Important

It is nothing new to say that the Bible, throughout the Old and New Testaments, says repeatedly that the attitude—the inward person—is the all-important element in true religion. The outward expressions that are prescribed by God are important. But without the proper attitude, the rigorous teaching and performance of right actions and precise beliefs do nothing but

sicken God's heart. The following passages emphasize this principle and could be multiplied in both the
Old and New Testaments.

In 1 Samuel 16:7, God said to Samuel as he
looked for the new king to replace Saul, "The Lord
does not look at the things man looks at. Man looks at
the outward appearance, but the Lord looks at the
heart."

In Psalm 51:16-17, David makes this confession after his encounter with the prophet Nathan over
the sin with Bathsheba: "The sacrifices of God are a
broken spirit; a broken and contrite heart, O God, you
will not despise."

Micah 6:8 phrases God's rebuke of Israel this
way: "He has showed you, O man, what is good. And
what does the Lord require of you? To act justly, to
love mercy, and to walk humbly with your God."

In response to his disciples' question concerning the greatest in the kingdom of heaven, Jesus said
in Matthew 18:3-4, "Whoever humbles himself like a
child is the greatest in the kingdom of heaven."

Paul gives a summation of moral precepts in
Romans 13:10 which is similar to that of Jesus in
Matthew 5. Paul says: "Love does no harm to its
neighbor. Therefore love is the fulfillment of the law."

Romans 14:4 -15:2 is filled with direction on
the kind of attitude we should have toward brothers
and sisters in Christ. 14:4: "Who are you to judge
someone else's servant?" 14:12-13: ". . . each of us
will give an account of himself to God. Therefore let
us stop passing judgment on one another. Instead,
make up your mind not to put any stumbling block or
obstacle in your brother's way." Especially note
14:19: "Let us therefore make every effort to do what

leads to peace and to mutual edification."

In 2 Timothy 2:14 and 2:24, Paul urges Timothy to warn his hearers against "quarreling about words; it is of no value and only ruins those who listen . . . the Lord's servant must not quarrel; instead he must be kind to everyone, able to teach, not resentful."

The familiar unity passage in Ephesians 4:2 has Paul urging the Ephesians (and us), "Be completely humble and gentle; be patient, bearing with one another in love. Make every effort to keep the unity of the Spirit through the bond of peace."

James 3:17-18 tells us the essential characteristics of the wisdom that comes from heaven: ". . . first of all pure; then peace-loving, considerate, submissive, full of mercy and good fruit, impartial and sincere. Peacemakers who sow in peace reap a harvest of righteousness."

Paul reminds Titus in 3:2 of what is good: ". . . to slander no one, to be peaceable and considerate, and to show true humility to all men."

Matthew 9:13 is a crucial passage. After being severely criticized by some Pharisees for eating with a group of tax collectors and sinners, Jesus told them, "Go figure out what this means, 'I desire mercy, not sacrifice.'" Jesus was quoting from Hosea 6:6, a scathing denunciation of Israel's sacrifices; correct in form but offered from corrupt and merciless hearts.

Obviously, scripture makes a difference between a person's moral attitude and his or her correct practice of religion.

Honestly answer this question: according to these and many other passages, which is most important—the right attitude or the right practice? The answer should be obvious. Remember the words quoted by Jesus: "I desire mercy, not sacrifice." Does that mean that correct belief and practice are irrelevant? Certainly not! But the Scriptures are quite plain about the essential foundation for correct beliefs and practices—humility, mercy, gentleness, love of peace, and forbearance. The attitude characterized by these traits does not result from mere human effort, though the will is certainly involved. Instead, it is attained by submission to God's Spirit and by crucifying our sinful natures (Galatians 5: 13-26). It is absolutely essential to realize that without these things, without the mind and attitude of Christ, there can be no correct belief or practice.

Restoration Leaders and the Mind of Christ

The religious reform movement led by Thomas and Alexander Campbell, Barton W. Stone and a host of others was concerned to place the proper emphasis on one's attitude. Barton Stone, in the "Last Will and Testament of the Springfield Presbytery," included a paragraph that willed "preachers and people [to] cultivate a spirit of mutual forbearance; pray more and dispute less. . ." Stone, in a classic article published in his *Christian Messenger* in 1835 declared

> The scriptures will never keep together in union and fellowship members not in the spirit of the scriptures, which spirit is love, peace, unity, forbearance, and cheerful obedience. This is the spirit of the great Head of the body. I blush for my fellows, who hold up the Bible as the bond of union yet make their opinions of it tests of fellowship; who plead for union of all Christians; yet refuse fellowship with such as dissent from their notions. Vain men! Their zeal is not according to knowledge, nor is their spirit that of Christ. There is a day not far ahead that will declare it. Such anti-sectarian sectarians are doing more mischief to the

cause, and advancement of truth, the unity of Christians, and the salvation of the world than all the skeptics in the world. In fact they make skeptics.[3]

In his famous "Declaration and Address," Thomas Campbell expressed similar sentiments and frustration with the division in the religious world of his day.

> . . . the first and foundation truth of our Christianity is union with [Christ], and the very next to it in order, union with each other in him. . . For this is his commandment: that we believe in his son Jesus Christ and love one another. . . But how to love and receive our brother, as we believe and hope Christ has received both him and us, and yet refuse to hold communion with him is, we confess, a mystery too deep for us. If this be the way that Christ hath received us, then woe is unto us. We do not here intend a professed brother transgressing the express letter of the law, and refusing to be reclaimed.

> [It is an evil] not only judging our brother to be absolutely wrong, because he differs from our opinions, but more especially, our judging him to be a transgressor of the law in so doing, and, of course, treating him as such by censuring or otherwise exposing him to contempt, or, at least, preferring ourselves before him in our own judgment, saying, as it were, Stand by, I am holier than thou.[4]

What is Our Attitude in Churches of Christ Today?

Surely none would disagree that if every member of Churches of Christ today had the mind or attitude of Christ, we would not be in danger of fragmentation. But consider such statements as the following taken from a recent brotherhood publication:

> While assuring the brotherhood that they believe in an inspired scripture, [the two brothers]

stalemated themselves by preaching a noxious modernistic "gospel." It should be apparent, from the manner in which their hobby generally persecutes holy writ, that this is only one phase of a blitzkrieg campaign to erase Biblical authority. Predictably [the two] denied such lethal linkage all the while annoying listeners with New Hermeneutical formulas and catch-phrases.[5]

Another brother is described as brainwashed. Nothing about his once wonderful reasoning processes seems, in the writer's opinion, to work anymore:

> . . . this once-reliable, erstwhile dependable stalwart for the truth has left no stone unturned to undermine the doctrinal principles that he formerly affirmed, going even into strange cities attempting to destroy the very churches of Christ with whom he once stood.

Later, this brother is described as a "muley cow" because he no longer had horns to hook with—that is, he would not enter into debate with the author. The author then declares that a forum several years ago marked the end of this brother's honorable defense of his convictions.[6]

Such attacks are not confined to one side in the current frictions. Conservatives, liberals, pietists, intellectuals, and almost every other group that might be identified has used inflammatory language at times in dealing with those with whom they disagree. This kind of language does not seem to demonstrate the mind of Christ. It is in no way kind, considerate, merciful, peacemaking or humble. Nor does the use of un-Christlike attacks on a brother or sister justify retaliation. Because someone else does not demonstrate the attitude of Christ does not make it right to reply in kind. Regardless of how sinful or bad someone might be, license is not granted for evil actions and words to combat them. Not everyone will have the mind of Christ, and even those who are trying to cultivate that attitude don't instantly have it in full measure. As Christians, however, we must always consciously submit to that mind.

Does having the attitude of Christ mean that we should not reprove or rebuke those who believe and act in ways contrary to Christ and his teaching? Obviously not. Paul instructed the Christians in Ephesus to reprove the unfruitful works of darkness (Ephesians 5:11). Paul told Timothy to rebuke an elder who sins publicly (1 Timothy 5:20) and to reprove, rebuke and exhort those in his charge with all longsuffering and doctrine, or, as the New International Version renders it, with "great patience and careful instruction" (2 Timothy 4:2). None of those passages or any other, however, overrides the overwhelming thrust of scriptural commands, exhortations and examples that Christians in all their dealings are to be characterized by the attitude of Christ, who submitted to the cross. Whatever it means to reprove and rebuke, nothing can negate that supreme scriptural imperative.

Conclusion

We are in the midst of a period of great stress in Churches of Christ; stress that has been building for at least twenty-five years. This decade will be a crucial one in our history. The one thing that will avert a major fragmentation is for each of us to cultivate the attitude of Christ in our dealing with brothers and sisters. That is God's plan for maintaining unity among his followers. The seeming dichotomy between humility and conviction is false. Having strong convictions need not result in a harsh, abrasive, hurtful and combative attitude—in fact, it *must* not.

In Romans 8:9, Paul informs the Roman Christians that they are not to be controlled by the sinful nature, but by the Spirit. And if anyone does not have the Spirit of Christ, he says, that person does not belong to Christ. Simple admonitions to humility are seldom enough to bring carnal humans to have the mind or attitude of Christ. Our worldly attitudes and elevation of self must be shattered before that mind can take hold of us. May God give us what we need so that each of us may have the mind, the spirit, and the attitude of Christ. May we all come to be known by our humility, mercy, compassion, love of peace and of each other. then the world will know, as our Lord prayed, that we are his disciples.

Endnotes

[1] Isaac Errett, *Christian Standard* 4 (July 3, 1869): 213.

[2] H. Leo Boles, "The Mind of Christ," *Gospel Advocate* 78 (October 29, 1936): 1034.

[3] Barton W. Stone, "Remarks," *Christian Messenger* 9 August 1835): 180.

[4] Thomas Campbell, *Declaration and Address* (reprinted. St. Louis: Mission Messenger, 1978), 55, 72-73.

[5] Bill Lockwood, "Another Hermeneutical Hopscotch: The Freed-Hardeman Forum, 1990, On 'The Woman's Role,'" *Contending for the Faith* 22 (April 1991): 1.

[6] Ira Y. Rice, "Woodmont Hills, Rubel Shelly

Refuse Knight Arnold Elders, Garland Elkins' Challenge to Debate Salvation Issue," *Contending for the Faith* 22 (June 1991):1; and Rice, "'Muley' Cows Do Not Believe In Hooking," *Contending for the Faith* 22 (June 1991):2.

Chapter 8

Case Study: The Example of T. B. Larimore

T he last quarter of the nineteenth century was a tumultuous period for the Restoration Movement, a period in which one major division took shape and was realized, and the roots of another division began to grow. Different individuals viewed the problem in different ways. Some believed the "conservatives" or "anti's" were trying to add terms of fellowship to those spelled out in the New Testament. Others believed the "progressives" or "digressives" had added unauthorized items to God's clear plans for evangelization and worship and had pushed these innovations upon many who had conscientious scriptural objections to them. Each side pointed the finger at the other as being responsible for the rapidly solidifying division.

There were a few individuals, however, who attempted to defuse this explosive environment and hold the Restoration Movement together. One of these

T. B. Larimore (1843-1929)

peacemakers was Theophilus Brown Larimore. Born in poverty and illegitimacy in upper east Tennessee on July 10, 1843, Larimore rose to become one of the movement's most widely known and best-loved evangelists in the late 1800's and early 1900's. He was baptized in Hopkinsville, Kentucky on his twenty-first birthday in 1864 while the Civil War continued to rage. From there he went to Franklin College near Nashville to study under A. J. and Tolbert Fanning, graduating as valedictorian of his class on June 6, 1867.[1]

Larimore was convinced of the usefulness of education and taught in Alabama and Tennessee before establishing Mars Hill Academy near Florence, Alabama, in 1871. He continued to operate the school six months out of the year until 1887.[2]

In 1875 Larimore, like many preachers, tried his hand at editing a paper. But Larimore's paper was different from the others. It was specifically designed to help stop the dissension and divisiveness becoming increasingly evident in the movement. He named the paper *The Angel of Mercy, Love, Peace and Truth*. In the first issue Larimore printed a "Greeting from the Angel" in which he set forth part of his editorial policy.

> I come, not in a dictatorial spirit, nor do I claim infallibility. No angel should be that presumptuous, for some have fallen. Being quite a youthful angel, myself, with very limited experience, I shall doubtless commit many blunders. However, they shall be "errors of the head, and not of the heart," and, as I am an independent angel, alone responsible for my utterances, you will please do not expose me, but help me all you can.

> Love, if there be such a dweller in your heart,
> will constrain you to do this; but if, being devoid of
> love, you make war upon me; and try to work my ruin;
> I shall neither defend myself, nor try to injure you. My
> master instructs me to love my enemies, and do good
> to those who despitefully use and persecute me. "I am
> for peace"—my *name* is Peace—and no word of bitter-
> ness shall ever fall from my lips, *even in self-defense.*

Later in the same issue Larimore declared that the *Angel* would carry in every issue "an appropriate notice of every one of our own periodicals." In essence it was a free advertisement for every paper published in the Restoration Movement. Included were the titles, editors, publishers, prices and addresses for over twenty papers, including the *Gospel Advocate, American Christian Review, The Christian, The Evangelist,* and *The Christian Standard;* papers covering the whole spectrum of positions on the various issues. Every month the notice appeared that one harsh, unkind or unpleasant word would be sufficient reason for consigning to the flames any article submitted for the *Angel's* pages.

The paper failed as a financially self-sustaining enterprise. The failure was due perhaps as much as anything else to Larimore's policy of allowing each subscriber to determine his or her own subscription price. The next year he tried again with a slightly revised format and a prepaid subscription price of $1.25, but that effort also failed, ending Larimore's editorial aspirations for a while. Some have speculated that the chief reason for the failure of *The Angel* was the fact that people did not want a paper that minimized the difficulties in the movement. The majority wanted a paper that would "get into the fight." Perhaps so. But Larimore had shown in this effort that one could promote Christ and gospel truth without battling with brothers and sisters; without calling names or drawing lines.

Two years after the closing of the Mars Hill school, an intimate friend, F. D. Srygley, wrote a book about Larimore's work of training preachers at Mars Hill, titled *Smiles and Tears; or, Larimore and His Boys.* Srygley wrote that all efforts to draw Larimore into controversy over the issues of the day had been unsuccessful. He then quoted from two private letters written by Larimore during his Mars Hill days that illustrate Larimore's approach to the matter of unity within the movement.

> I do not pitch into my brethren who do not do exactly as I do, or understand everything just as I do, for two reasons: 1. I can understand how it is possible for them to act correctly and still not always do exactly as I do. 2. I love my brethren, and, long, long ago solemnly resolved never to go to war with them, or, rather, against them. It seems to suit some good brethren to dispute with each other; but it does not suit me. They may be able to do much good in that way, but I believe I would do great harm and no good if I should attempt it. I love some of my brethren better than others, and admire the ways of some more than others; but I hate none of them. I love them all, and am unchanged and unchangeable in my determination never to dispute with any of them, or basely suspect any of them of evil motives and designs.

> I propose to keep my face to the common foe as long as life lasts, but to never try to down a brother. If falsely accused and harshly assailed, publicly or privately, I propose to undertake neither explanation, retaliation, nor defense. I am determined to follow our Savior's example as nearly as I can, and I think he never tried to avenge himself. If I live as I should live, my life will sufficiently vindicate me; if not, I ought not to be vindicated. So then, in any event, it is both useless and sinful for me to undertake to vindicate or avenge myself. This is settled, in my mind, and, as a necessary and natural result, many other things are settled too.[3]

Larimore experienced tremendous success in his evangelistic work. F. D. Srygley said near the turn of the century that Larimore had baptized more people and established more churches than any other person in the Restoration Movement then living. At his death it was estimated that he had baptized over 10,000 persons.[4]

But all was not well. It was exasperating to many that Larimore refused to line up with any side in the developing split. He continued to do what he had always done—preach the simple gospel message of salvation to any and all who would have him. This course prompted some harsh criticism from all sides in the fights of his day, but he refused to defend himself and would not be drawn into the divisive conflict.

Larimore's five-month meeting at Sherman, Texas in 1894 illustrates the tensions he was dealing with. The Houston Street Church in Sherman had been troubled by division over the missionary society in 1882, and when Larimore was asked to come for a meeting in 1894 the instrumental music issue was threatening to divide the congregation again. During the time Larimore was there, however, peace prevailed. He never so much as mentioned the instrument, yet over 200 were baptized, the instrument which had been in the building was moved out, and at the end of the meeting the church asked Larimore to be its regular minister, which he refused.[5]

Before the year was out, however, the progressives and conservatives were meeting at separate times, and the next year the pro-instrument faction withdrew to form what they called the First Christian Church. The Dallas *Christian Courier,* a progressive journal, evidently angry that Larimore would not endorse the instrument, began to accuse Larimore of having sown dissension in the Sherman church while he was there. Larimore, as was always his practice, did not utter a word in defense. F. D. Srygley and the *Gospel Advocate* came to Larimore's defense, showing that the problems were there long before Larimore had come. But the editorial battle continued, off and on, for two years, and many of the pro-instrument churches in Texas boycotted Larimore for a time; something that hurt him deeply and which he never quite got over.[6]

Voices from all sides continued to pressure Larimore to reveal which part of the movement he sided with. He always responded that, as far as he knew, he belonged to nothing except that to which every Christian belonged—the church. "I have never belonged to a 'wing' of the church or anything else. I belong to Christ, hence to the *church* of Christ—not to a 'wing' of the church," he stated. The factions in the movement were identified by their stands on the questions of the day. Tongue in cheek, Larimore suggested that these questions were not good things to stand on. If Christians thought they had to do something with the questions, it would be better to sit on them, and to stand on Christ and him crucified.

In 1897 an exchange took place in which Larimore was pushed to declare himself publicly on the various divisive issues. This was done through the medium of an "open letter" to him published in several of the brotherhood papers. Oscar P. Spiegel, a former pupil of Larimore's at Mars Hill and then State Evangelist for Alabama, wrote:

It is not best, in my humble judgment, to be silent when we see our fellow men, and especially our own family, drifting apart. Thousands of your friends believe you owe it to yourself, your family, your friends, your Saviour and your God to speak out on some matters now retarding the progress of the cause of Christ . . . Please therefore, answer the following questions according to your judgment:

1. Is the use of an organ, or other instrument of music, in connection with congregational singing, permissible in the Lord's house, and does its use do violence to the teaching of God's Holy Word?
2. Is organized mission work permissible?— by which I mean an organization, or organizations, other than the local congregations?
3. Are conventions, consultation meetings, mass meetings, cooperative meetings—or whatever one chooses to call them—to which disciples come at their own expense from congregations in a given county, district, state, or nation, antagonistic to, or in harmony with, the scriptures?
4. Is regular monthly, semi-monthly, or weekly preaching by one who is giving himself "continually to prayer and the ministry of the word," conducive to the best interests of the cause of Christ, or derogatory thereto?
5. Is a *quid pro quo* contract, either verbal or written, between a preacher and a church, or churches, for and with which he labors, in harmony with the scriptures, or contrary thereto?
. . . thousands of your brothers and sisters believe it is your duty to speak out on these questions, and strive to unite, if possible the people of God. And surely when duty calls you will respond.[7]

Larimore's response was lengthy—so lengthy that J. H. Garrison, editor of the *Christian-Evangelist,* complained he had to leave out several good articles to print it all. But print it he did, as did the editors of the *Gospel Advocate* and *Christian Standard.* Larimore quickly cut to the heart of the enquiry.

To which—or *what*--party do *I* belong in this unfortunate controversy? "That's the question." Had I "spoken out" on "matters" mentioned in your "open letter," this question had never arisen; for *all* had known. Your letter is proof positive, then, that you and . . . THOUSANDS of other friends before whom "my life is an open book" believe I have never "spoken out," have never expressed an opinion or a preference—on ANY of these things. THAT IS TRUE. NEVER, publicly or privately, have I expressed opinion or preference relative to ANY of these "matters" . . . over which brethren are wrangling and disputing and dividing the church of Christ—NEVER. . . . I am sorry to disappoint any of my friends; but it is *certainly* clearly my duty, to . . . leave the discussion of all such questions to wiser, better, abler men, and just simply "PREACH THE WORD," avoiding, always, all questions that "do gender strifes" among the children of God. Wiser and better men do otherwise, however, and some good brethren may deem it their duty to denounce, renounce, criticize, censure, condemn, boycott and abuse me, and refuse to recognize, fellowship or affiliate with me, because I am as I am, do as I do, and, *especially*, because I have written *what* I have written in answer to your "open letter." I shall *certainly* never retaliate. I shall simply do as I have ALWAYS done: *"love the brethren"*; be true to my convictions; endure as patiently as possible whatsoever may come upon me; go when and where I am wanted and called, if I can; carefully avoid all questions that *"do gender strifes"* among God's people; "PREACH THE WORD"; *try* to do MY WHOLE DUTY, and GLADLY leave ALL results with HIM from whom all blessings flow.[8]

Larimore did continue to preach the Word wherever he was called; but, while his name remained on the List of Preachers in the Disciples Yearbook until 1925, the number of calls from churches in that fellowship gradually shrank to nothing. Hundreds in Christian Churches, however, including his own sister Mollie, continued to love and respect him. He was asked to write the obituary of David Lipscomb for the *Christian Standard,* and maintained as many contacts with converts, friends and former pupils in Christian Churches as he was able. When Larimore died in March, 1929, articles of tribute appeared in all the major Disciples journals, and the number of articles that poured into the *Gospel Advocate* spilled over into most of three issues.[9]

Two points about Larimore's life are especially relevant to our current predicament. The first can be seen in an exchange that took place concerning Larimore between the *Christian Standard* and the *Gospel Advocate* in 1946.

Seventeen years after Larimore's death, S. S. Lappin, editor of the *Christian Standard*, wrote and published two articles about T. B. Larimore and his non-partisan, non-sectarian spirit, especially focusing on his great success as an evangelist. Lappin emphasized that Larimore did not enter into the fractious controversies of his day, referring to the troubles as "the long and foolish controversy about instrumental music in worship and the missionary societies."[10]

Lappin's articles appeared in June. In October G. C. Brewer wrote an article for the *Gospel Advocate* titled "A Letter to Brother Lappin About Brother Larimore." Brewer basically agreed with the *Christian Standard's* statements concerning his mentor, but he wanted to add some facts to the accounts, particularly concerning the 1894 Sherman, Texas meeting. Brewer concluded his article by saying:

> "[Larimore] was in no sense a partisan, and he never spoke evil of any man, but he did have firm convictions; and notwithstanding the fact that his own brother-in-law, Rufus Meeks, went with the brethren who introduced instrumental music, Brother Larimore never departed in the least from the position held by all the brethren prior to the introduction of these things."[11]

G. C. Brewer was exactly right. Although, as Larimore himself said on several occasions, he never publicly declared himself on the issues because he was too busy "preaching the Word," others, including David Lipscomb, said that Larimore did have convictions concerning the matters, and these convictions most certainly included opposition to the innovations.

And that is precisely the point! To Larimore those issues were not worth dividing the body of Christ. While he held conservative beliefs about them, he felt that they were "untaught" questions, that is, the Bible did not mention them. It was his duty as a Christian and an evangelist to preach Christ and the clear teachings of the New Testament and to have nothing to do with questions, as he said, over which the wisest and best of men disagreed.

In a 1917 *Gospel Advocate* article Larimore wrote:

> I never call Christians or others "anti's," "digressives," "mossbacks," "tackies," or "trash." I concede to all, and accord to all, the same sincerity and courtesy I claim for myself, as the Golden Rule demands. . . .

> Can a man who simply preaches the word wheresoever he goes and whensoever he preaches, and always stands behind that proposition, be justly accused, or even suspected, of being responsible for discord, dissension, division or strife among the children of God? If all of us would reduce that proposition to practice, would we not necessarily, become and be one, thus fulfilling the Lord's prayer? If some of us refuse to do this, thus preventing the fulfillment of that sacred prayer, who of us are guilty? It is a fearful thing to bear such a burden of guilt as that. Of the seven things Solomon declares to be an abomination unto God, the crown of the climax is "he that soweth discord among the brethren." (Prov. 6:19) So then, my brother here are my head, my hand, my heart, for peace, for

scriptural peace, for honorable peace, for universal peace, for permanent peace, among all the children of God, the Bible being the basis; hence for the final fulfillment of the Lord's prayer for Christian oneness...[10]

Someone once told me that if everyone had had T. B. Larimore's attitude toward the problems facing the church in his day, the church would have been completely lost to false doctrine. This statement begs the question. The fact is that if everyone had had T. B. Larimore's attitude, the problems would never have been blown up into divisive issues in the first place. T. B. Larimore's life is a model of how God's plan for unity is supposed to work. To his eternal credit, that is his greatest significance, and his lasting contribution to our fellowship.

Endnotes

[1] Biographical information was gleaned from the so-called "Larimore books" which include F. D. Srygley, *Smiles and Tears; or, Larimore and His Boys* (Nashville: Gospel Advocate Pub. Co., 1889); F. D. Srygley, ed., *Letters and Sermons of T. B. Larimore* (Nashville: Gospel Advocate Pub. Co., 1900); Emma Page, ed., *Letters and Sermons of T. B. Larimore,* vol. 2 (Nashville: McQuiddy Printing Co., 1904); vol. 3 (1910); Mrs. T. B. Larimore (Emma Page Larimore), ed., *Life, Letters and Sermons of T. B. Larimore* (Nashville: Gospel Advocate Co., 1931).

[2] See T. B. Larimore, "Greetings from the Golden Gate: Mars Hill Memories," *Gospel Advocate* 69 (May 19, 1927):467-8.

[3] Srygley, *Smiles and Tears*, pp. 230-231.

[4] Wayne W. Burton, "Unique Career in Church History," *Gospel Advocate* 71 (May 16, 1929):473-4.

[5] See the account in Stephen Daniel Eckstein, *History of the Churches of Christ in Texas, 1824-1950* (Austin, Texas: Firm Foundation Publishing House, 1963), 186-190.

[6] See "From the Papers," *Gospel Advocate* 36 (August 2, 1894):475-6; (September 6, 1894):555-6 and Lloyd Cline Sears, *The Eyes of Jehovah: The Life and Faith of James Alexander Harding* (Nashville: Gospel Advocate Company, 1970), 86.

[7] O. P. Spiegel, "Open Letter to T. B. Larimore," *Christian Standard* 33 (July 10, 1897):891.

[8] T. B. Larimore, "Reply to O. P. Spiegel's Open Letter," *Christian Standard* 33 (July 24, 1897):965-67.

[9] See especially the May 16, 1929 "Memorial" issue of the *Gospel Advocate.*

[10] S. S. Lappin, "T. B. Larimore--Effective Gospel Evangelist," *Christian Standard* 82 (June 22, 1946):421-22; "T. B. Larimore, Evangelist--Who Fought a Good Fight," *Christian Standard* 82 (June 29, 1946):438, 448.

[11] G. C. Brewer, "A Letter to Brother Lappin About Brother Larimore," *Gospel Advocate* 88 (Ocotber 17, 1946):982-3.

[12] T. B. Larimore, "The Bible is the Basis," *Gospel Advocate* 59 (March 15, 1917):253-4.

Will the Cycle be Unbroken?

Chapter 9

Following the Leaders:
Where Are They?

In our past it was often possible for the entire movement to acknowledge common leaders. People like Alexander Campbell, David Lipscomb, and Batsell Barrett Baxter set a tone for the churches. Not everyone always agreed with them, yet each in his own lifetime commanded the respect and support of a broad constituency. Each was a person able, in the words of Gary Wills, to "mobilize others toward a goal shared by leader and followers."[1] Presently no such common leaders exist among us.

Some lament that there simply are no great leaders anymore. "If only we had someone like J. W. McGarvey or David Lipscomb we might be able to recover the unity and drive we once had," they opine. The problem, however, is not necessarily a lack of leaders. As Wills points out in *Certain Trumpets: The Call of Leaders,* the roll of follower is the crucial one. In his definition of a leader quoted above, there must be a shared goal—a joint quest—toward which a leader takes others. Leaders cannot lead without followers.

> Followers judge leaders. Only if the leaders pass that test do they have any impact. The potential followers, if their judgment is poor, have judged themselves. If the leader takes his or her followers to the goal, to great achievements, it is because the followers were capable of that kind of response. Jefferson said the American people responded to revolution in a way that led to a free republic, while the French responded to their revolution in a way that led to imperial dictatorship. The followers were as much to blame for the latter development as was Napoleon.[2]

Perhaps this chapter should be asking: what kind of followers do we have in Churches of Christ today? Leaders, good or bad, are powerless without followers. By looking at whom we choose as leaders, we can see into our own souls.

Often our leaders have been prominent traveling evangelists, college presidents, and journal editors—those in control of the institutions described in chapter four. Some have been spiritual leaders of the highest caliber. Others have caused great problems for the churches. The leadership role that receives chief attention in Scripture, however, is that of the congregational elder. It is here that we begin talking about leadership in the church.

Elders in Old Testament Times

Elders in ancient times rose from the ranks of the senior members of what we would call extended families. Tim Willis, in a study of elders in Old Testament times, identifies five of their basic characteristics: (1) they were senior members of large and respected extended families; (2) they were generous and hospitable; (3) they were an example of their society's highest standards of ethics and morality; (4) they were well-versed in their people's religious knowledge, customs and history; and (5) they were known for their skills of teaching and persuasion.[3]

The same kinds of characteristics were true of Israel's elders (see Job 29) and of the elders described for the "extended families" of Christians in 1 Timothy 3 and Titus 1. Willis concludes, "Paul's prescriptions for elders were nothing new to the world. The characteristics Paul gives are, in fact, typical of elders in most tribal societies."

Paul was not giving a business plan for successful management. He was trying to create a community out of people who had been unrelated, but who were now related in a special and intimate way in a new kind of extended family. The elders were not a governing board or in charge of an administrative structure. They were respected senior members of a community, a family of believers.

Elders in the New Testament

The New Testament uses at least three terms to refer to the persons recognized as the spiritual leaders of communities of believers. The term "elder," from the Greek *presbuteros*, refers primarily to the person's age. Yet it meant more than simply having lived many years. This Christian was more experienced and wiser than others in the family, commanding respect and love.

"Bishop," from the Greek *episkopos,* carries the idea of guardian or overseer—though that second word may produce images that are foreign to the biblical sense of the term. It is not the image of a slave's overseer, watching to discourage slackers and giving the lash to those who get out of line. It has, rather, the idea of one who watches out for others, who protects them from harm, who takes up for them in times of conflict.

The third term is "pastor" or "shepherd." This image expresses the idea that the spiritual leader does what a shepherd does—that is, he establishes relationship with the sheep from the time they are little lambs. They know the shepherd and the shepherd knows them. The shepherd feeds them and protects them, leads them to green pastures and still waters, and wins their responsiveness by laying down his life for the sheep.

The Historical Development of Church Leadership

Very early in church history there were important developments in the way the leadership was organized. By the end of the first century some churches had a threefold ministry made up of (1) deacons, (2) elders or presbyters, and (3) a head elder or bishop who presided over the meetings and the operations of the church.[4] By the end of the second century this pattern had become the norm. Eventually all aspects of leadership that had belonged to the group of congregational elders had been taken over by the bishop.

This change was partially in reaction to threats from false teachings, such as gnosticism, faced by the primitive church. How could one be sure that the doctrines of groups like the gnostics, who claimed to have special teaching from Jesus and the apostles, were not true? People came to believe that the bishops constituted the link with the earliest church, with Christ and the apostles. The truth had come to them in an unbroken succession that went back to Christ himself. They were the superintendents of the truth and the judges of all heresy.

After the Roman emperors legalized Christianity and made it the state religion, the bishops enjoyed new prestige and power. They came to be known as "the princes of the Church" in the Middle Ages, often wielding the same power as the princes of the world.

Church Organization in the Reformation

The sixteenth-century reformers strongly attacked abuses of the office of bishop. Not all of them were opposed to the office itself, however. The Church of England and parts of the Lutheran movement, for example, kept the office of bishop. Others, especially the Reformed tradition of Ulrich Zwingli and John Calvin, had the goal of going back to the Bible and reinstituting what they understood as biblical leadership. Instead of ordained bishops that were successors of the apostles, "lay" elders from every congregation should govern, they believed.

Calvin conceived of four offices in the church: preaching ministers, teachers, deacons and elders. Elders had oversight of the spiritual needs and the lives of the members of the congregation. Calvin understood that elders were to be chosen by the church, serving by the consent and recognition of the congregation. This had been taken away in the Middle Ages by the Roman hierarchy. To be more biblical, the Calvinists instituted these forms that became known as presbyterianism, after the Greek word for elder, *presbuteros.*

The English Church kept the medieval office of bishop. A major grievance many English Puritans had against the Anglican Church was that it lacked New Testament organization. English Baptists were especially concerned with going back to a New Testament model of leadership. These people were considered the most radical of all the Puritans because they insisted on separation of church and state. In the London Confession of Faith, adopted by the English Baptists in 1689 and by the Baptists in Philadelphia in 1742, these radicals proclaimed that

> A particular church, gathered and completely organized according to the mind of Christ, consists of officers and members; and the officers appointed by Christ to be chosen and set apart by the church, . . . are bishops, or elders, and deacons.
>
> The way appointed by Christ for the calling of any person, fitted and gifted by the Holy Spirit, unto the office of bishop or elder in a church, is that he be chosen thereunto by the common suffrage of the church itself; and solemnly set apart by fasting and prayer, with the imposition of hands of the eldership of the church, if there be any before constituted therein . . . .[5]

Both Presbyterians and Baptists understood Scripture to distinguish between two kinds of elders: ruling elders—those who made judgments in congregational matters of discipline—and teaching elders—those who were responsible for instructing the congregation from the Word. In practice, both Presbyterian and Baptist churches in America came to view the elder chosen to instruct the congregation as *"the pastor."* Yet all their statements of belief continued to include the idea of a plurality of bishops or pastors in every congregation.

The Restoration Tradition

Both the Presbyterian and Baptist branches of the Reformation influenced our own heritage in the Restoration Movement. Thomas and Alexander Campbell were members of the (Presbyterian) Associate Synod, a faction of the Church of Scotland. Barton W. Stone was ordained in the Presbyterian Church in the United States of America. Soon after the Campbells broke from the Presbyterians in the early 1800's, they associated themselves with the Baptists for fifteen years. Alexander Campbell preached as a Baptist, defended adult immersion for them in several debates, and named his first paper *The Christian Baptist*.

In 1825 Alexander Campbell began a lengthy series of articles in *The Christian Baptist* titled "A Restoration of the Ancient Order of Things." Articles 12, 13 and 14 dealt with "The Bishop's Office." Two ideas stand out strongly in Campbell's early teachings on elders. First, he insisted that they be qualified to teach. While not every elder was to devote his full time to the ministry of teaching, some should. In line with the Baptist practice, many early preachers in the Restoration Movement were called "elder" because of their role of teaching and preaching.

Second, contrary to most religious leaders from a Reformed background, Campbell preferred the term "bishop" to describe congregational leaders. "Elder" was simply a designation of age, he insisted, and was inadequate as a description of the leader's function. The term "bishop," on the other hand, described a function—overseeing. "It implies a good and arduous work."[6]

In 1830 Campbell began a new journal called the *Millennial Harbinger.* In 1835, in a special issue of the *Harbinger,* Campbell again addressed the matter of church order and leadership. He pointed out that a congregation of Christians guided by the Word in selecting their bishops was in reality simply recognizing what the Holy Spirit of God was doing among them. He quoted Acts 20:28, "Take heed to yourselves and to the whole flock over which the Holy Spirit has made you bishops."

Campbell went on to say that in cases where there were no elders already in place, those chosen should be formally appointed or ordained by the representative laying on of the hands of the whole congregation. He also gives a lengthy description of how the eldership should prepare cases to present to the entire congregation when a member has been accused of some wrongdoing. His description is reminiscent of a presbyterian-style church trial, except that the entire congregation was to be in on the proceedings.[7] Eventually the norm for congregations in the Restoration Movement was to have elders along the model of the "ruling elders" of the Presbyterians and Baptists, with a sharp distinction made between elders and the "minister" or preacher.

Churches of Christ

As we saw in chapter six, toward the end of the nineteenth century, American society went through a period that one historian has called "the incorporation of America."[8] American society as a whole accepted the ideals of centralization, organization and efficiency. These ideas changed the way people thought about all of life, including the churches.

American denominations developed centralized headquarters with strong bureaucracies and increasing
numbers of agencies. The Christian Churches and
Disciples centralized their ministries until they consol-
idated the missionary and benevolent organizations
into the United Christian Missionary Society. Even
in the Churches of Christ, the eldership was increasingly perceived to operate as a corporate board of
directors. The "authority" of elders became a prominent issue in the late 1800's.

Some, like David Lipscomb and E. G. Sewell,
resisted this new corporate model of church leadership. They insisted that the notion of "office" in the
church did not mean a position that conferred power
as it did in the world. Such an idea was a misunderstanding of the word "office" as it appeared in 1 Timothy 3:1 in the English translations then used. (For
example, the American Standard Version says "If a
man seeketh the office of a bishop, he desireth a good
work.") They insisted the verse simply meant that
anyone who desires overseeing desires a good work.
The New International Version translates the verse,
"If anyone sets his heart on being an overseer, he desires a noble task."

As for the authority of elders, Lipscomb wrote

> All the authority [elders] possess in any mat-
> ter is the moral weight their wisdom and devotion carry
> with them, gained through obedience to the will of God,
> and the express declaration that they and all of God's
> servants must be respected in doing the works assigned
> them by the Holy Spirit.[9]

The biblical notion of office, Lipscomb insisted, simply meant duty—the obligation to do a certain work. The way to become an elder was by doing

the work of an elder. The congregation then recognized the work by conferring together. When that happened, the Holy Spirit had already appointed them elders, and the congregation had merely recognized the accomplished fact.

All decisions for the church should be made, Lipscomb believed, by the church as a whole. The elders were to voice the decision by conferring with all the members, even the most humble. They were not to make arbitrary rulings based on their perceived authority.[10]

One of the most prominent teachers opposing Lipscomb's ideas of leadership was J. W. McGarvey of Lexington, Kentucky. In a short book titled *A Treatise on the Eldership,* McGarvey insisted that "elder" was an *official* position in the church, that elders had authority from God to rule the church, and that they, in their capacity as teachers, are judges of the law in every case of disorderly conduct. Yet even McGarvey conceded that the designation of shepherd is the most explicit and most important term used for the elder, and that it would be inconceivable that an eldership would not know the sentiments of the congregation before making any decision.[11]

This matter has continued to be a concern through the twentieth century. In the 1950's and 1960's, the focus of questions concerning church leadership turned to the authority of elders. As in the late nineteenth century, some saw the elder as an officer of the church endowed with authority. Others rejected any notion of authority at all to describe the nature of elders' leadership.[12] Among those who rejected a legal authority for elders were Reuel Lemmons, editor of the *Firm Foundation*, Jack Lewis, teacher at

Harding Graduate School of Religion, and J. W. Roberts of Abilene Christian. The other position was represented by B. C. Goodpasture and Guy N. Woods of the *Gospel Advocate*, and preacher Roy Lanier, Sr.

One of the most lively exchanges over this matter took place when Reuel Lemmons wrote an editorial in the August 2, 1977 issue of the *Firm Foundation*, titled "Who Calls the Shots?"

> . . . someone needs to challenge the growing "authority" syndrome. . . . We are aware that Paul told the Ephesian elders to "feed the church over which the Holy Spirit had made them overseers," but to use this to make elders governors is to use the passage wrongly. There is a difference in overseer and commander. Peter put it well when he said, "Feed the flock of God with is *among* you. . . ." There was no chiefs-and-Indians syndrome in the New Testament church.
>
> The problem of lordship has long been with us. Jesus' disciples argued over who should have the preeminence. Who would call the shots? At that very point Jesus told them that if any of them would be great they must become a servant of all.[13]

This sparked many replies, both pro and con, for several months. Lemmons published many of the responses that took issue with him in the *Firm Foundation*. Roy Lanier, Sr. focused on passages like Hebrews 13:17 where the language is that of *obeying* those who *rule* over you, with the command to *submit* to them. He insisted that simply because some elderships had abused their authority, it did not negate that authority. Lanier ended, however, on the same note as Lemmons. Any eldership that did not consider the wishes of the members in decisions was both "unwise and inconsiderate. They really are not fit to be elders."[14]

As mentioned in chapter six, Jack P. Lewis, in his 1985 book *Leadership Questions Confronting the Church*, conducted a thorough study of every New Testament word used for the nature, work and characteristics of elders. No passage, he concluded, connected the idea of "authority" to the eldership. Instead, the emphasis was on sacrifice and service, on "doing a good work." Christians were to esteem elders as stewards of God.[15]

While there are differences in these concepts of leadership, there are some understandings that predominate. Elders are experienced Christians, wise and deserving of respect. They are pastors, bishops, and shepherds who lead and protect the flock. They do not appoint themselves nor are they appointed by a board of elders without the clear acceptance of the congregation. They are shepherds—servants of the Chief Shepherd, and not members of a corporate board of directors. As such, the well-being of individual people, not the "corporation," becomes the most important thing. They must love, nurture and discipline the members of the congregation. Their primary function is not decision-making in a traditional business sense. It is leading and feeding in a spiritual sense. The role of the shepherd is perhaps best pictured, not in Timothy or Titus, but in Matthew 18:12-14.

> If a man owns a hundred sheep, and one of them wanders away, will he not leave the ninety-nine on the hills and go to look for the one who wandered off? And if he finds it, I tell you the truth, he is happier about that one sheep than about the ninety-nine that did not wander off.

Leadership for Our Current Crisis

There are hundreds of books on the market today that describe effective leadership styles in dozens of ways. The way Scripture describes leadership begins with Christ's statement in Mark 10:42-45:

> Jesus called [his disciples] together and said, "You know that those who are regarded as rulers of the Gentiles lord it over them, and their high officials exercise authority over them. Not so with you. Instead, whoever wants to become great among you must be your servant, and whoever wants to be first must be slave of all. For even the Son of Man came not to be served, but to serve, and to give his life as a ransom for many."

This passage describes what Lawrence Richards and Clyde Hoeldtke call the "command" and "servant" models of leadership.[16] Our culture places emphasis on authority, decision making, and control. Leaders expect obedience and see themselves as above their followers. A middle style, called the "sharing" model, places leaders and followers side by side. Each helps sustain the other.

It is the servant model, however, that best reflects the language of Scripture in passages like Ephesians 5:1-2 and Philippians 2:5-8. In this model, the leader "voluntarily chooses to spend himself on behalf of the other and makes it his goal to nurture, support, and build up the one with whom he is in relationship."[17] This kind of leadership is, even among the people of God, very rare. This kind of leadership is what we must have to break the cycle of division.

If we have the goal of becoming like Christ, both individually and as a church, we as followers must seek out leaders who can, with God's power, lead us toward that goal. If, on the other hand, our goal is denunciation of brothers and sisters, strife, and division, we will choose leaders who promise to lead us to such ends. True Christian leaders must be able to discern both what the church has become and what, with God's help, it should be. Christian leadership, in the words of David Wells, "is a matter of teaching and explaining what has not been so well grasped, where the demands of God's truth and the habits of the culture pull in opposite directions."[18] The habits of culture pull us toward conflict and separation from those with whom we differ. What we often have failed to grasp is that the message of Christ does just the opposite.

How can we find the leaders and be the followers we must to break the cycle of division? Consider the inspired words of Paul:

> Be imitators of God, therfore, as dearly beloved children, and live a life of love, just as Christ loved us and gave himself up for us as a fragrant offering and sacrifice to God (Ephesians 5:1-2).

Endnotes

[1] Gary Wills, *Certain Trumpets: The Call of Leaders* (New York: Simon & Schuster, 1994), 17.

[2] Ibid, p. 21.

[3] Tim Willis, "Functions of Elders in the Old Testament Community," Paper presented at the Christian Scholars Conference, July 20, 1988, Pepperdine University.

[4] See for example the writings of Ignatius in Polycarp 6 and Smyrneans 8.

[5] *The Philadelphia Confession of Faith*

(Reprint ed., Gallatin, Tennessee: Church History Research and Archives, 1987), 64.

[6] Alexander Campbell, "A Restoration to the Ancient Order of Things. No. XIII. The Bishop's Office.—No. II, *Christian Baptist* 3 (June 5, 1826):214. References to the *Christian Baptist* are from the Gospel Advocate reprint edition, 1955.

[7] Alexander Campbell, "Order," *Millennial Harbinger—Extra* 6 (October 1835):493-507.

[8] Alan Trachtenberg, *The Incorporation of America: Culture and Society in the Gilded Age* (New York: Hill and Wang, 1982).

[9] David Lipscomb, "Officers and Officialism in the Church of God," *Gospel Advocate* 9 (July 18, 1867):568.

[10] See C. Leonard Allen, *Distant Voices* (Abilene: ACU Press, 1993), 100-106.

[11] McGarvey, J. W., *A Treatise on the Eldership* (Cincinnati: Bosworth, 1870; reprint ed., Murfreesboro, TN: DeHoff Publications, 1950), 9-15.

[12] See Tim Willis, "The Office of Elder in Church of Christ Publications, 1950-1980," Paper presented at the Christian Scholars Conference, David Lipscomb University, July 20, 1991.

[13] Reuel Lemmons, "Who Calls the Shots?" *Firm Foundation* 94 (August 2, 1977):482.

[14] Roy H. Lanier, Sr., "The Eldership," *Firm Foundation* 94 (November 15, 1977):724. See also David L. Desha, "Elders and Authority," and Dub McClish, "Reply to 'Who Calls the Shots,'" both in the same issue.

[15] Jack P. Lewis, *Leadership Questions Confronting the Church*, (Nashville: Christian Communications, 1985), 34.

[16] Lawrence O. Richards and Clyde Hoeldtke, *A Theology of Church Leadership* (Grand Rapids: Zondervan, 1980), 24.

[17] Ibid., 25.

[18] David F. Wells, *No Place for Truth; or, Whatever Happened to Evangelical Theology?* (Grand Rapids: William B. Eerdmans Publishing Company, 1993), 215-16.

Chapter 10

Restoration:

God's Finished Work--

Our Never-Ending Quest

What we need in Churches of Christ is restoration. When we hear that term, most of us think of the nineteenth-century American effort to reestablish New Testament Christianity begun by Barton Stone and the Campbells. But ask a group of modern Roman Catholics and they will explain that restoration consists of Rome's attempt to return to the rigid, dogmatic Catholicism of the era before the 1960's and Vatican Council II.[1] Question a gathering of Latter-Day Saints and they will tell you that Joseph Smith began the Restoration with his 1830 discovery and translation of the *Book of Mormon*.[2] Query members of the Universalist Church of America (now part of the Unitarian-Universalist Association), and they will inform you that it means the eventual restoration of all people to fellowship with God in heaven.[3]

The notion of restoration is not as easy to pigeonhole as some might expect. Restorationism assumes a sharp break between the way things are now and the way things used to be or ought to be. The vision of exactly what to restore and how to do it varies with different times and cultures. All restoration movements, however, seek to make things "right again."

True Christian restoration focuses on areas in which the church has departed from its intended ideal in belief and practice, weakening its relationship to God and his power. Spurred by prophetic voices that challenge the comfortable and self-satisfied, restoration movements often call for radical change. Barton Stone called for a fundamental restoring of the life of the Spirit evidenced by the fruits of Galatians 5. Alexander Campbell urged people to tear themselves away from their denominational connections to take a simple, rational approach to the New Testament Scriptures. Like all restoration efforts, both experienced rigorous opposition.

Restoration, at its heart, is the work of God. Restoration is what he has done and what he will do to restore what he intended for us from the foundation of the world (Ephesians 1:4; 2 Timothy 1:9). We tend to see restoration primarily as a human effort, but nothing could be farther from the truth. Humans did not devise a way to restore the relationship with God which was broken by our sin—God did. Centered on the sacrifice of Jesus Christ, his plan is surely unfolding in human history.

Scripture uses the term to speak of God's restoration of Israel after Babylonian captivity (Deuteronomy 30:3; Jeremiah 16:15) and his restoration of all things at the end of time (Acts 3:21). It also urges the gentle restoration of individuals by godly, spiritually mature Christians (Galatians 6:1). Humans respond by accepting or rejecting God's work. Even when we accept his will, our part of the process of restoration will never be final until we are made perfect in Christ after this life. As we grow in reliance on God's unbounded grace, as we continue to "walk in the light," Jesus' blood must continually do its restoring work (1 John 1:7). As individual Christians and together as Christ's church, we must be engaged in a never-ending quest to grow up in Christ.

James O. Baird makes a helpful distinction between the terms "restoration," "restoration principle," "restoration ideal," and "restoration movement." Restoration is the continuing process by which God's actions and human response bring people "back" into a proper relationship with God. This happens either through discovery of and action on previously unknown truth or returning to a proper relationship with God after having left it. The restoration principle is the idea that people, motivated by love and fear of the righteous God, seek to restore their relationship to him, willing to respond however God wants. The restoration ideal revealed in the Bible is the standard of God's will to which we aspire. The deep need to restore a right relationship with God (the restoration principle) points us toward his will (the restoration ideal). Finally, the "restoration movement" points to the human, corporate aspect of the discussion. The Stone-Campbell restoration movement is one historic attempt to seek the restoration ideal.[4]

The Stone-Campbell Restoration Movement was and is a collective attempt by godly women and men to submit their lives and thought to God's will. In its beginnings, historical and cultural situations influenced the ideas and conclusions of its founders. They differed on many things, including the exact nature of restoration itself. They were united, however, in the desire to restore a right relationship to the God of Scripture. We are grappling today with many difficulties that arise from our own historical and cultural contexts. The only thing that can unite us, despite our differences, is a similar commitment to relationship with God.

Accounts of restoration efforts fill the pages of church history. Alfred T. DeGroot, in a book titled *The Restoration Principle*, identified dozens of such efforts from the earliest days of the church to the modern era. Among those from ancient times he mentions the Montanists of the late second century. This group sought to restore the urgent expectation of Christ's second coming, chaste and simple living, and the importance of prophecy in the work of the church. They believed they were restoring New Testament Christianity in its uncorrupted form, rescuing it from an increasingly institutionalized church. In the ninth century a book written by an unknown author, titled *The Key of Truth,* denounced the apostasy of the state church and described the simple faith, order, worship and life of a true church patterned after the example of the apostles. The fourteenth-century leader John Ruysbroek sought to restore primitive Christianity in the spirit and tenor of the Christian's life, rather than merely in external forms.[5]

The Dukhobors of Russia were sometimes erratic, but broke with the Russian Orthodox Church in the seventeenth century in search of simple primitive Christianity.[6] John Wesley's eighteenth-century reform movement sought to return to the doctrines and practices of ancient Christianity. When the Revolution cut American Methodists off from the English Church, Wesley told them they were "simply to follow the Scriptures and the Primitive Church."[7] The Scottish restoration movements begun by John Glas, Robert Sandeman, the Haldanes and others, though differing in important specifics, all pointed to Scripture alone as authority in religion and to the "restitution" of New Testament Christianity.[8]

England's Puritans promoted the restitution of primitive Christianity, as did the Anabaptists of the continental Reformation. Furthermore, the Holiness and Pentecostal movements of the late nineteenth and early twentieth centuries claimed to be restoring the spiritual gifts characteristic of the primitive church, as opposed to mere doctrinal formulations or church structures.[9] These are samples of the many attempts to restore Christianity to its ideal as conceived by the restorers.

Historically, restoration movements have shared several problems. First, they are selective in their vision of what to restore, each tending to conclude that its restoration effort embraces all that is valid in true Christianity.[10] Second, restorationists too often make peripheral issues central to their message. None has devised a simple program of "distinguishing majors from minors," a fact contributing to restorationism's reputation for divisiveness.[11] In our own history, divisions have occurred over issues as diverse as the use of Sunday Schools, multiple cups in the Lord's Supper, located preachers, and support for parachurch organizations like orphans homes and the Herald of Truth. Third, the initial impetus and fervor of restoration efforts generally wane and take a different

181

shape after the first generation. Movements often move far from the intentions of their founders.

These problems are rooted in the fact that we are human, and human efforts are fraught with such liabilities. Perhaps the problems result from our failure to focus on the primacy of God's action in restoration. Human response is involved, but restoration is not our work—it is God's. Only by constant reaffirmation of our submission to his will and through the guidance of his word and spirit can such tendencies be tempered.

Several new efforts openly claim restorationist intent. *Christianity Today* recently featured a charismatic restoration movement that uses house churches to evangelize. Its adherents believe that "the modern church has lost the power, patterns and spiritual gifts of the New Testament Church, all of which can and should be recovered."[12] Their teachings include that the church is the kingdom of God today (as opposed to dispensational premillennialism), that elders who act as spiritual shepherds are to govern the church, and that there is a biblical pattern of worship.

"Open Church Ministries," also known as "The Seedsowers," led by James Rutz and Gene Edwards, sees itself as a restoration of early Christianity. The group's letterhead proclaims: "Aiding the Restoration with pure worship, true sharing, free ministry." The movement emphasizes truly restoring the "priesthood of the believer" so that all Christians are active participants, rather than spectators, in worship and ministry.[13]

Though every restoration effort has its idea of precisely what needs restoring, two consistent emphases are apparent: (1) the restoration of one or more precise biblical doctrines, practices or structures, and (2) the restoration of a spiritual life manifested in daily ethical actions. These are not mutually exclusive. Doctrine is intimately connected with and necessary to a relationship with Jesus Christ. Yet doctrine must result in more than merely having right understandings and precise formulations in the believer's head. The *point* of doctrine is Christ—it points us to Christ, our savior and example. Restoration of correct doctrine is not the end. True restoration must result in a life characterized by a proper relationship to Christ; a life distinguished by Christ's humility, his love, his righteousness and his selfless concern for others. This, as we have seen, is God's prescription for unity. Restoration and renewal are not mechanical human processes. They involve our deepest spiritual existence; they require being led by the Spirit of God (Galatians 5:18). Furthermore, any attempt to restore correct doctrinal knowledge that produces un-Christ-like attitudes and conduct is a perversion of true doctrine and a fundamental misunderstanding of Christianity. "The letter kills, but the Spirit gives life" (2 Corinthians 3:6).

The biblical imperative to contend for the faith cannot be understood as a charter to destroy fellow Christians. When ridicule and the attribution of vile motives become typical, we have entered Satan's realm. Barton Stone perhaps said it best when he insisted that unity would be restored only on a spiritual foundation.

> But should all the professors of Christianity reject their various creeds and names, and agree to receive the Bible alone, and be called by no other name but Christian, will this unite them? No: we are fully

convinced that unless they all possess the spirit of that book and name, they are far, very far, from Christian union.[14]

Churches of Christ must not focus on maintaining a status quo, but on the never-ending pursuit of the restoration ideal. Only with God's help can we avoid the extremes of either harsh and rigid over-emphasis on doctrinal precision or sentimental relativism that refuses to seriously pursue God's ideal. The unsettling, prophetic voices among us will not go away, nor should they. As individual Christians and as a church we must bow to the will of God. We must pray that he will indeed restore us to him and transform us into a new creation.

Endnotes

[1] Penny Lernoux, *People of God: The Struggle for World Catholicism* (New York: Viking Penguin, Inc., 1989).

[2] See for example Steven L. Shields, *Divergent Paths of the Restoration: A History of the Latter Day Saints Movement* (Bountiful, UT: Restoration Research, 1982), and Milton Vaughn Backman, *Eyewitness Accounts of the Restoration* (Salt Lake City, UT: Deseret Book Company, 1986).

[3] See for example Elhanan Winchester, *The Universal Restoration* (Philadelphia: Gihon, Fairchild & Co., 1843); Kenneth M. Johnson, *The Doctrine of Universal Salvation and the Restorationist Controversy* (Bangor, ME: Kenneth M. Johnson, 1978).

[4] James O. Baird, "Denial of the Validity of the Restoration Principle," *Gospel Advocate* 134(February 1992):20-21.

[5] Alfred T. DeGroot, *The Restoration Principle* (St. Louis: The Bethany Press, 1960), 93, 94, 108.

[6] Ibid., 130.

[7] Cited in Ted Campbell, *John Wesley and Christian Antiquity* (Nashville: Kingswood Books, 1991), 51.

[8] Lynn A. McMillon, *Restoration Roots* (Dallas: Gospel Teachers Publications, Inc., 1983).

[9] See C. Leonard Allen and Richard T. Hughes, *Discovering Our Roots: The Ancestry of Churches of Christ* (Abilene,TX: ACU Press, 1988), 35, 125, 137.

[10] DeGroot, *The Restoration Principle*, 45, 133.

[11] Thomas Olbricht, "Biblical Theology and the Restoration Movement," *Mission Journal* 13(April 1980):4.

[12] Garry D. Nation, "The Restoration Movement," *Christianity Today* 36 (May 18, 1992):27.

[13] James H. Rutz, *The Rebirth of the Church* (Auburn, ME: The Seedsowers, 1992), 10.

[14] Barton W. Stone, "Christian Union," *Christian Messenger* 3 (December 1828):37-38.

Will the Cycle be Unbroken?

The Promise of Spiritual Renewal

Two things are necessary to break the cycle of division in Churches of Christ. They are clearly inseparable, but they are different. First is individual revival; that is, spiritual renewal that alters lives and individual outlooks and transforms behavior. The Bible teaches that such a change involves absolute submission (Romans 12), the breaking of the arrogant human will, and acknowlegement of God's all-powerful nature, of our sinfulness and utter helplessness.

Our tendency as humans is to become more and more arrogant, particularly those of us who enjoy good educations, jobs, and comfortable lives. We may submit to a number of regulations and obligations, but we believe we remain in charge of our lives. God, we assume, is the one who steps in and makes up any difference after we have done almost everything required. Changing such a secular worldview is almost always a jolting life experience; one which causes a radical re-evaluation of old ways of thinking and acting.

The second necessity, a result of the first, is an awakening in the entire fellowship of the Churches of Christ. Revivals or awakenings occur when large numbers of individuals have their thinking radically changed—when they are converted from an old way of thinking to a new one. Such awakenings typically begin, according to sociologist William McLoughlin, "in periods of cultural distortion and grave personal stress, when we lose faith in the legitimacy of our norms, the viability of our institutions, and the authority of our leaders."[1] In other words, spiritual renewal takes place when large numbers are jolted into realizing that they are not in charge—that they must rely on the One who created us and who longs for a relationship with us.

It is possible to resist the Spirit, however (Acts 7:51). If we do not see the need for spiritual renewal; if we are comfortable with the way things are going, there will be no breaking the cycle of division.

Whatever position we might take on the issues, wherever we may fall on the spectrum, surely we would all say that we do not want division. And regardless of the feelings we may hold toward those who do not agree with us on the troubling matters, surely we can all pray for unity—without allowing our own agendas to intrude. Remember the admonition of James: "Confess your sins to each other and pray for each other so that you might be healed." (James 5:16) Remember the words of our Lord: ". . .all things are possible with God" (Mark 10:27).

A reversal of our path to division can come

only if we earnestly pray for such a change. Recently, a poster advertising a southern religious school came to my attention. It carried a photograph of a young man kneeling to pray, with the caption

> Even when they disagree, Christians should share the same position. Where there's disagreement, there's reason for prayer. Because in the humble search for God's answers we find understanding. So before you take a stand for what you believe, spend some time on your knees.

May God draw us closer to him every day. May he create in us a heart of love for each other. May he raise up servant leaders in our congregations and in our nation who will lead us toward the unity Jesus prayed for. May his Spirit guide us in our words and actions, and may those actions reflect the Spirit's fruit in our lives. May our pride be destroyed and our zeal be renewed as we work together with God. May we become the living proof of Paul's words to the saints in Rome: "You are not controlled by the sinful nature but by the Spirit, if the Spirit of God lives in you" (Romans 8:9).

Endnotes

[1] William McLoughlin, *Revivals, Awakenings, and Reform* (Chicago: The University of Chicago Press, 1978), 2.